About the author

John Simpson has been a keen student of steam engines for over seventy years, part of an eventful career that includes photography, gliding, and scientific research. At Cambridge in the 1930s he was President of the Railway Club. Two significant events for him were the arrival of the Flying Scotsman, and discovery of three Manning Wardle industrial locomotives within cycling distance. During World War II he worked with the Friends Ambulance Unit in China. Even there he was able to photograph steam engines on the metre gauge railway near Kunming. Returning to England, he first taught physics, and then had a long spell at the Department of Applied Mathematics and Theoretical Physics at Cambridge where he wrote definitive books on Gravity Currents and Sea Breeze. In his world travel, he came across many preserved steam locomotives, often the product of Manning Wardle & Co. Thus began his study of the famous Leeds firm of engine builders.

Locomotives of Quality

A Pictorial History
of
Manning Wardle & Co.

John E Simpson

Ross-Evans

British Library Cataloguing in Publication Data

Simpson, John E
Locomotives of Quality: a pictorial history of Manning Wardle & Co.
1. Manning Wardle & Company – History
2. Steam Locomotives – History – Great Britain
I. Title
385.3'61'0941

ISBN   1 874498 02 4

Printed by
The Burlington Press
1 Station Road, Foxton, Cambridge

Published by
Ross-Evans
St. Mary's House, 47 High Street, Trumpington,
Cambridge CB2 2HZ

PREFACE

As an enthusiastic photographer of locomotives of light railways and industrial locomotives in the 1930s, I came across some very fascinating engines. Finding a new Manning Wardle was always a red-letter day - all those from the Boyne Engine Works in Leeds had a special magic about them.

In recent years I found that I was not alone in this special interest, and that other people were striving to preserve the few remaining examples, both in this country and in other parts of the world. So, gathering together my own old photographs, I began to study more carefully the products of this famous Leeds firm of engine builders.

Starting from my personal exploration as an enthusiast over a period of seventy years, I was fortunate to have the added help of some distinguished railway photographers and experts on the subject. I discovered how the products of this famous Leeds firm developed, and how their locomotives spread all over the world. Lastly I tried to find all the Manning Wardle engines that have been preserved, and in many cases brought back to working order.

This personal tribute to Manning Wardle inventiveness has been prepared in the hope that other enthusiasts will enjoy following my illustrated story of their remarkable locomotives, what they did, where they went, and how to find those that have been preserved.

John Simpson
Cambridge
October 2000

ACKNOWLEDGEMENTS

As well as those who have contributed Manning Wardle pictures, I owe a special thanks to three helpers. These are Dick Riley, railway photographer, who gave me the choice of over one hundred photographs; Ronald Redman, railway-man and author, for his painstaking work in checking the manuscript; and Philip Atkins, Librarian of the National Railway Museum who greeted me with a large table piled head-high with Manning Wardle material. I wish to thank all those who have so willingly helped me to assemble this book, and my daughter Ann for the design of the cover.

CONTENTS

Preserved locomotives

CHAPTER ONE

Foundations of the Company

Industrial locomotives in Leeds

The history of the industrial locomotive started in earnest in Leeds. John Blenkinsop of the Middleton Colliery was looking for alternative power because of the increased cost of horses and fodder caused by the Napoleonic Wars, lasting until 1815. Doubtful of the adhesion of smooth wheels, Blenkinsop had patented a rack-rail system and turned to Matthew Murray to build him a steam locomotive using his patent. Fenton, Murray & Wood built this first engine in their general engineering workshops in 1811, as recorded on pottery at the time.

Figure 1.1 The Blenkinsop locomotive, from a water-colour by George Walker. (published in 'The Costumes of Yorkshire' in 1814)

The success of this locomotive showed that the Blenkinsop rack-drive was the right answer to the problem of the cast iron rails of the time. The contemporary sketch in figure 1.1 shows that, like the earlier Trevethick engine, it was driven by levers and gears, but also included another feature that was an important technological advance. This was the use of two cylinders working at right angles to each other instead of the one that needed a heavy flywheel, as in Trevethick's engine. There was a toothed wheel on the axle that fitted into the toothed rail mounted alongside the running rails.

Two more locomotives followed in 1812, named *Prince Regent* and *Salamanca*. Four more of these engines worked successfully for many years and two were also constructed in 1813 for the Kenton & Coxlodge colliery, Newcastle. They were able to haul a load of ninety-four tons on the level at three-and-a-half miles per hour, proving themselves the first commercially successful engines in the world.

Matthew Murray was not concerned with developing the steam locomotive business, as he was far more interested in mill-engines and such like. In fact he even produced at least one riverboat engine for use on the Mississippi.

During the following fifteen years a number of successful steam engines were built by several constructors. However the design did not alter much, and even Stephenson's *Locomotion No.1* which drew the first steam train on a public railway was not very different in design.

Fundamental changes in design of the steam locomotive came in 1829 when Stephenson's *Rocket* was built for the famous Rainhill Trials. The *Rocket* was in many ways the prototype of the modern steam locomotive. Three important features were:

1   The multi-tubular boiler in which the heat was transferred to the water through a large number of separate tubes.
2   A suitable shaped blast pipe.
3   A change to a simple power transmission, using a direct rod to the driving wheel.

Fenton, Murray & Jackson: The Round Foundry

After the death of Matthew Murray in 1826, his place in Leeds was taken by his son-in-law Robert Jackson, and the firm of Fenton, Murray and Jackson started building locomotives. In a short time they became the first commercially successful locomotive builders, carrying out subcontracting work for Robert Stephenson, notably on locomotives of the Planet type 2-2-0. One of these is illustrated in figure 1.2 and shows that the design has come a long way since the Blenkinsop engine.

The original textile factory expanded at the plant at Holbeck and gained the name *The Round Foundry*. Among the many successful orders completed were a series of twenty 'Fire Fly' class broad gauge 2-2-2 express engines, built for David Gooch of the Great Western Railway.

Figure 1.2 The first *Planet* locomotive.
(from a drawing by G.H. Phipps, Wood's 'Treatise on Rail Roads', 1831).

E.B. Wilson & Company: the Railway Foundry, Hunslet

When Fenton, Murray & Jackson went out of business in 1843, many of their former employees were looking for work in the locomotive construction business. Previously, a group had started building railway engines in the district of Hunslet in southeast Leeds. Todd, Kitson & Laird set up their first locomotive works in Hunslet in 1839, but the firm soon broke up, and out of this developed two groups. Kitson & Laird started building locomotives at the Airedale Foundry which developed into the large and successful Kitson & Company. On the other side of the road, Shepherd and Todd had a small works that later became the Railway Foundry.

This firm built locomotives until 1846 when it was taken over by Fendon, Craven & Company. After less than a year, E.B.Wilson became manager and the business of E.B.Wilson & Company of the Railway Foundry was formed. This neighbourhood was eventually to include, as well as Manning Wardle, the other three firms of Hudswell Clarke, Kitsons, and the Hunslet Engine Company.

Figure 1.3 The 2-2-2 Express *Jenny Lind*,
built by E.B.Wilson at the Railway Foundry in 1847.

E.B.Wilson was a remarkable man, and during his reign of just over ten years built up a very successful locomotive business. As soon as he came to power he started an ambitious programme of expansion and built a large area of new workshops. He pioneered the standardisation of design and early semi-mass production in the age of light main-line locomotives, even building up stock for quick sale. The Railway Foundry's most successful and famous design was the *Jenny Lind* Express 2-2-2 (figure 1.3). The prototype, designed by David Joy, had the unprecedented boiler pressure of 120lb per square inch and was most impressive with her polished strip mahogany boiler lagging, and dome and safety valves with fluted centres and square bases. She performed so well that Matthew Kirtley of the Midland Railway ordered six engines on the spot; and at one time the factory was turning out one of these engines a week.

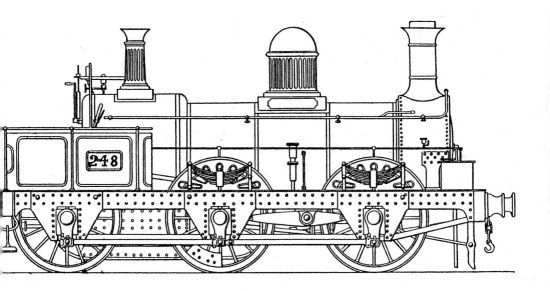

Figure 1.4 0-6-0 locomotive built by E.B.Wilson in 1854.
One of the many built of this type, this example became No. 248 of the Great Western Railway.

Wilson built over six hundred engines for use in Britain and overseas, and made a noteworthy contribution to locomotive history. Many of these were inside cylinder double-framed 0-6-0 engines, and over one hundred and sixty were built to a standard design (figure 1.4). All had the distinctive fluted domes and safety valves that had become a Wilson trade mark.

By 1856, Wilson had become at odds with his shareholders and he made his final departure from the Railway Foundry. Alexander Campbell was then appointed manager for the last years of the company's existence, during which the feud continued and the company was finally wound up in 1858. By this time Campbell and others had taken steps to safeguard their future. Joining forces with C.W.Wardle and John Manning they acquired five-and-a-half acres of adjacent land from the estate of Lord Boyne to form the Boyne Engine Works which traded under the name of Manning Wardle and Company.

Growth of factories in Hunslet

No buyers were found for the major lots into which the Railway Foundry land had been divided and all the buildings were pulled down. By 1858 the Boyne Engine Works occupied a small plot adjoining the original Railway Foundry Estate, and during the following ten years all the rest of the estate came to be occupied by locomotive builders.

As Manning Wardle expanded along Jack Lane, the next new engine works established were that of Hudswell & Clarke in 1860. They filled the former lot 6 between the railway line and the pottery works on the west side of Jack Lane, and were named the New Railway Foundry.

In 1864, yet another company was formed. Mr. John T. Leather was a contractor who saw the increasing demand for industrial locomotives and formed the Hunslet Engine Company. This was on the land adjoining that of Manning Wardle, on the same side of Jack Lane.

So by this time, there were four locomotive manufacturers in Hunslet, all adjoining each other. In order of foundation these were: Kitsons, Manning Wardle, Hudswell Clarke, and Hunslet.

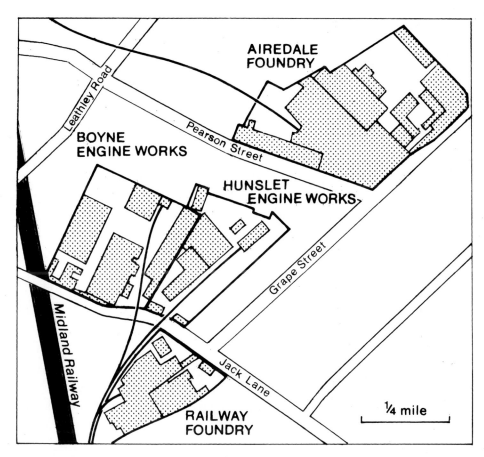

Figure 1.5 Map of the four locomotive manufacturers in Hunslet.
(based on Ordnance Survey of 1888.)

All around these locomotive works were crowded dwellings in a maze of back-to-back terraced houses. The workers had to live close to their place of work as there was not yet any public transport for them.

In the Ordnance Survey Map of 1888 (figure 1.5) the four locomotive manufacturers can clearly be identified.

The Airedale Foundry	Established 1835 by Todd, Kitson, Laird who, after varied partnerships, became Kitson & Co. in 1863.
Boyne Engine Works	Established by Manning Wardle & Co., 1858.
Railway Foundry (new)	Hudswell & Clarke & Co., 1860.
Hunslet Engine Works	Hunslet Engine Co., 1864.

Manning Wardle & Company: The Boyne Engine Works

When the Railway Foundry was put up for sale, Manning Wardle purchased the drawings for seventeen types of E.B.Wilson locomotives. This continued to influence their products in the early years, and features of Wilson engines can be seen in their locomotives.

The very first locomotive completed was a four coupled saddle tank of 3ft gauge, *Little Nell*, built for the Sheepbridge Ironwork in Chesterfield. The next two, works numbers 2 and 3, were 2-4-0T built for the Portuguese National Railway, the first of many export orders that were to follow. Also included in the first ten built were three of Wilson's famous express engines of the *Jenny Lind* type.

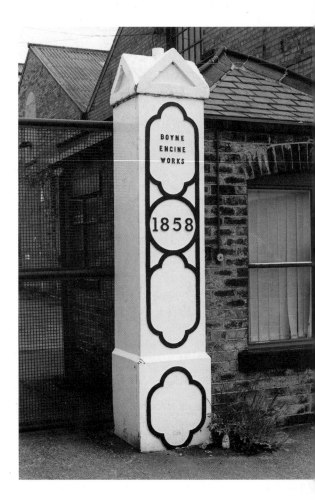

Figure 1.6 The cast iron gatepost of the Boyne Engine Works, (photograph by the author in 1996).

As well as selling *Jenny Lind* express locomotives to Australia and exporting many other different types, they soon made a name for themselves as suppliers of contractor locomotives.

Manning Wardle also supplied many locomotives for standard gauge branch lines and light railways. These will be seen later in the book; but one of the earliest, still with Wilson-like features, is shown in figure 1.7. This is 2-4-0T, *Brewster*, no. 34 of 1861, one of three built for the Colne Valley & Halstead Railway.

Figure 1.7 *Brewster*, 2-4-0T, MW no. 34 of 1861,
as originally received by the Colne Valley & Halstead Railway.
(photograph National Railway Museum.)

These locomotives show the characteristic fluted dome and safety valve covers of the Wilson era. Manning Wardle also imitated the Railway Foundry's engraved rectangular number plates (figure 1.8). These plates can just be detected on the plinths of the domes of the early locomotives.

Engraved   Brass   23⅝" x 5⅞"

Figure 1.8 Early Manning Wardle engraved rectangular number plate,
based on the Wilson design.

In the early 1870s, an oval plate was adopted. At first this was engraved, but later a
version with raised letters was introduced. Figure 1.9 shows one version of the oval
number plates.

Figure 1.9 Manning Wardle oval number plate.
(photograph Colin Wilson)

The company built up a very good reputation and continued to build locomotives at the Boyne Engine Works in Leeds from 1859 to 1926. During this time they produced many different types, but their name is especially linked with small industrial engines of distinctive appearance.

Photographs of the Boyne Works with men or 'shop' views are very rare, so figure 1.10 is of special interest. It shows *Henry Woodcock* on steam test outside the erecting shop doors with a suitable gang of fitters, sporting a nice collection of flat cloth caps.

Figure 1.10 MW no. 1717 of 1907, 3ft 10ßn gauge, 0-4-2ST, *Henry Woodcock,*
built for the Low Moor Iron Co., on steam test at the Boyne Engine Works.
(photograph R.N.Redman Collection)

Manning Wardle locomotive works list

The locomotive lists of all the products of Manning Wardle have been preserved and an example of two facing pages is shown in figure 1.11. As well as the works number and date, details of the engine are given, and finally the date and destination are shown. Further details sometimes appear as later history, such as when an engine is returned for heavy repairs or any orders for spare parts.

LIST OF LOCOMOTIVE ENGINES BUILT AT

ORDER No.	MAKERS' No.	DESCRIPTION OF ENGINE	Fire Box	Tubes	Boiler Plates	Axles	Tyres	Tried in Steam
2320 / 2381	573	12" Class H	Bilby	Broughton	Taylors	Coopers	Bessemer	1875 Nov. 15
2320 / 791	574	12" " H	"	"	"	"	"	
2320 / 2945	575	12" " H	"	"	"	"	"	1876 Jany 31
2400 / 400	576	10" Special F	"	Broughton	Taylors	Coopers	Bessemer	1875
2440	577	8" " D	.	Elliotts	Cooper	"	"	Nov. 8
2540 / 2540	578	12" Special H	"	Broughton	Bowling	Bowling	"	
2550 / 2550	579	6" "	"	Elliotts	Farnley	Taylors Steel	Vickers Steel	1875 Dec. 1
2600 / 2600	580	12" Special H	"	Broughton	Taylors	Coopers	Bessemer	1876 Jan 21
2620 / 2620	581	15"	"	"	"	Taylor	"	Jany 3
2640 / 2	582	13" M	"	"	Cooper	Cooper	"	May 1
2640 / 2649	583	13" M	"	"	"	"	"	Aug 1
2700	584	10" F	"	Broughton	Taylors	Coopers	Bessemer	Feby 1
2700	585	10" F	"	"	"	"	"	June 5

THE BOYNE ENGINE WORKS, LEEDS.

Sent away	NAME OR NUMBER	OWNER	DESTINATION	
1875 Nov 25	No 997	N. E. Railway Coy	Hull	✓
1876 Jany 12	Fox	~~Stocksbridge Rly Coy~~	~~Deepcar~~	✓
Aug 9	Inflexible ~~MANCHESTER~~	~~J. P. Edwards~~ ~~S. Walter~~ Wm Rigby & Coy	Blaenau Festiniog ~~Manchester~~ nr Stoke on Trent	✓
1876 Oct 27	25	Norwegian Trunk Rly	Christiania	576
Nov 8	Beatrice	~~North & Hendre Lead Mining~~ ~~Gupper & Bayliss & Coy~~ ~~Bamford & Son~~ ~~Bradding & Mathear~~	~~Benfield~~ ~~Boyshorn~~ ~~Hull~~ ~~Burton on Trent~~	
June 13	Kirkstall Forge	Kirkstall Forge Coy	Kirkstall	✓
1875 Dec 13	Florence	Dick, Kerr & Co Ld ~~Hook Norton Ironstone Partnership Ld~~ ~~Duke of Sutherland~~	Surbeth Bambram ~~Brora N.B.~~	
1876 Jany 26	No 1	Bates Stokes & Coy	Liverpool	✓
Feby 7	Gunner	Cartner Kellner Alkali Co. Ld. ~~Secy of State for War~~	Weston Point nr Runcorn Royal Arsenal ~~Woolwich~~	3 ✓
May 19	No 3	Frodingham Ironstone Mines Rowland Winn ~~Ministry of Munitions of War~~	Frodingham	
Aug 7	Ciceter ~~Bucclose~~ ~~Barrowghook~~ ~~Radcliffe~~	~~J. H. Scott &c~~ ~~&c Braddock~~ ~~Hallam~~	~~Brmskier~~ Manchester	
Feby 21	Derby	Barnstone Blue Lias Lime Co ~~Bolton & Woolwich~~	Barnstone Nottingham	
July 3	No 6	~~Kirk & Randall~~ Kirk & Parry S. Williams & Sons	Norwich Dagenham Dock	

Figure 1.11 Extract from Manning Wardle locomotive works list.

The number of locomotives that were manufactured, indicated in five year periods, is illustrated in figure 1.12. The first hundred were produced by 1863 with the thousand mark being reached by 1887.

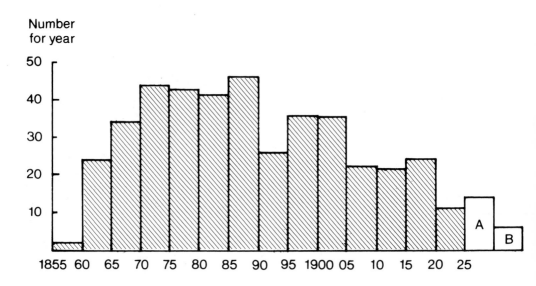

Figure 1.12 The number of locomotives built by Manning Wardle, shown in five year periods. Sections A and B were built by Kitson & Co and Robert Stephenson & Hawthorns, respectively.

One reason for the success of Manning Wardle was that, during the whole of their existence, all workers were employed by the hour and no parts were made on a piece-work basis. This certainly made for uniformly good workmanship; but after the First World War, this hand-built policy was one of the reasons why Manning Wardle began to have financial difficulties. At last, in 1926, after two thousand and four steam locomotives had been built, they were closed, and the goodwill and drawings went to Kitsons.

Kitson made twenty-three to Manning Wardle design, receiving Kitson works numbers. When the Airedale Foundry was also closed in 1938, patterns and goodwill were passed on to Robert Stephenson & Hawthorns who built a further five Manning Wardle type locomotives.

This was the end of Manning Wardle & Co. whose 'locomotives of distinction' worked in all parts of the globe. Fortunately many of them have been preserved, some even in working order, and these are described in the final chapter.

Figure 1.13 The last locomotive built by Manning Wardle & Co.,
0-6-0ST, no. 2047 of 1926, at the Rugby Cement works in 1966.
(photograph R.C.Riley)

CHAPTER TWO

Industrial Locomotives

0-4-0 Saddle tank engines

The saddle tank engine in figure 2.1 has an interesting history and could serve as a model for the family of Manning Wardle industrial saddle tanks.

La Portena was built by E.B.Wilson in 1856 and a popular legend has built up about her history. It is said that she was a broad-gauge veteran of the Crimean war, originally built for service on a British-owned railway in India. The legend says that after they had used the locomotive during the siege of Sevastopol, the British sold the worn-out locomotive to the Buenos Aires Western Railway for scrap iron. Recent studies have proved this account fictitious and it seems likely this story resulted from an attempt by Argentine Nationalists to stir up anti-British feeling during the 1890s. The venerable *La Portena*, which pulled her first train in 1857, was on prominent display during the 1948 ceremonies when the railway was handed over to Argentina. She is still preserved in Buenos Aires.

La Portena shows the domeless boiler which was one of the characteristics of E.B.Wilson's early tank engines. In place of the dome, the fire-box casing was raised a foot above the boiler barrel to provide a space from which the steam was taken. This form of raised fire-box casing was used for many years by Manning Wardle in their locomotives. Other features that were copied from Wilson designs were the square-sided saddle tanks and the smokebox door hinged at the top.

The early Manning Wardle locomotive in figure 2.2 is the class E, 0-4-0ST *Eva*, works number 213, built in 1866. She was so thoroughly rebuilt in 1879 that she was given the new works number 736, one of only four Manning Wardle locomotives to receive such a new number after rebuilding. Probably the rebuilding was so drastic that the resulting locomotive was virtually new.

Figure 2.1 2-2-OST, *La Portena*, built in 1856 by E.B.Wilson for the Buenos Aires Railway. Seen here at the Railway Exhibition, Retiro Station, Buenos Aires in 1968. (photograph R.N.Redman Collection)

Eva arrived at Petter's of Yeovil in 1920 with another legend about her origin. The story was that Ernest Petter bought a big pile of scrap metal in France after the First World War and later found *Eva* inside it. The generally accepted true story is that under the name of *Stafford*, she started work with William Moss, contractors of

Stafford. Next she went to Lucas and Aird, where she was renamed *Boyne* (after her maker's works) and then in 1911 was sold to Dixon & Carter Ltd of Northam.

In 1920 she moved to Petters where she acquired the name *Eva* on a brass nameplate with polished raised letters. When I took this photograph in 1934 she was nearing the end of her life in the siding at Yeovil.

Figure 2.2 *Eva*, MW 0-4-OST, works no.213 of 1866.
(photograph by the author in 1934 at Petter's works, Yeovil)

Figure 2.3 MW no.1084 of 1888, class H, at Greening & Sons at Warrington.
(photograph B.D.Stoyel)

Figure 2.3 shows a locomotive fitted with the original simple weather board, which was later extended to form a cover over the engine-men. It also shows clearly how much higher the firebox was above the main boiler.

Table 2.1 shows the typical dimensions of the Manning Wardle 0-4-0ST as they increased in size. Both the cylinder dimensions and the boiler size doubled during the years.

Table 2.1 0-4-0ST dimensions

Class	Wheel Diameter	Cylinders inches	Boiler Diameter	Length	Heating Surface sq ft	Tank Capacity gallons	Weight
B	2ft 6in	6 x 12	1ft 11in	6ft 9in	100	200	-
C	2ft 6in	7 x 12	1ft 11in	6ft 9in	125	200	8tons 10cwt
D	2ft 8in	8 x 14	2ft 1in	7ft 0in	177	200	9tons 18cwt
E	2ft 9in	9 x 14	2ft 3in	7ft 3in	248	250	12tons 5cwt
F	2ft 9in	10 x 16	2ft 7in	7ft 11in	300	350	15tons 3cwt
H	3ft 0in	12 x 18	2ft 9in	8ft 3in	364	450	19tons 10cwt
I	3ft 0in	13 x 18	2ft 10in	9ft 4in	472	500	-
P	3ft 0in	14 x 18	3ft 1in	9ft 4in	550	550	-

Figures 2.4 to 2.11 show eight more standard Manning Wardle 0-4-0ST. These all have outside cylinders, and include classes E, F, G and H. The different cabs seen

in some of these examples illustrate the kind of home-grown ones which were built
to replace the original basic Manning Wardle design.

Figure 2.4 MW no.653 of 1877, *Cameronian*, class F,
Burt, Boulton and Haywood at Southampton.
(photograph by the author)

Figure 2.5 MW no.786 of 1881, class E, Metropolitan Water Board at Lea Bridge.
(photograph Locomotive Publishing. Company)

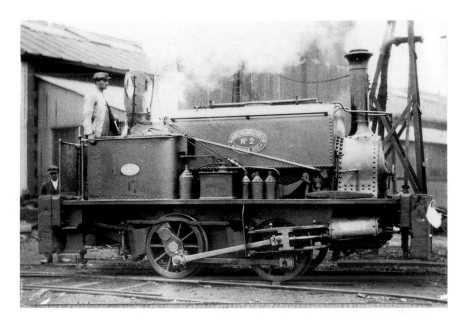

Figure 2.6 MW no.883 of 1883, No.2, class F, Samuel Williams and Son, Dagenham Dock.
(photograph R.C.Riley)

Figure 2.7 MW no.1023 of 1887, *Peterstone*, class H.
Formerly Staveley Coal and Iron Co. Ltd, then to Chesterfield Steel Breaking and Dismantling.
(photograph R.C.Riley)

Figure 2.8 MW no.1381 of 1899, class E, Bedford County Council.
(photograph by the author)

Figure 2.9 MW no.1549 of 1901 *Wyncliffe*, class E, Fishguard & Rosslare Railway, sold by GWR.
(photograph R.C.Riley Collection)

Figure 2.10 MW no.768 of 1881, class E 0-4-0ST, Metropolitan Water Board, Lea Bridge in 1932 (photograph F.J.Agar)

Figure 2.11 MW no.1846 of 1914, *Felspar*, class H, George Cohen & Son, Canning Town. (photograph B.D.Stoyel).

0-6-0 Saddle tank engines

Figure 2.12 0-4-2ST built by E.B.Wilson, no.387 of 1853, Oxford, Worcester & Wolverhampton Railway, later renumbered 221 by the Great Western Railway.

The standard 0-6-0 saddle tank engines built by Manning Wardle were inside-cylinder design, as opposed to the standard 0-4-0ST which had outside cylinders. The ancestors of the E.B.Wilson design appear to be two small saddle tanks built for the Oxford, Worcester and Wolverhampton railway in 1853. This design, which was actually a 0-4-2ST, had a short tank on the barrel only, with a domeless boiler and raised firebox (figure 2.12).

Like the 2-2-0ST *La Portena*, which led to the 0-4-0ST, these 0-4-2ST resulted in the K class 0-6-0ST. The early examples had the fluted safety-valve casing and the rectangular number plates of the Wilson era.

This class of 0-6-0ST became the most popular of all Manning Wardle locomotives and was exported to every part of the world. It was said to be an indestructible machine that stood up to rough treatment for years on end. About twenty of this type existed in 1997, some of them still in working order.

Table 2.2 shows the typical dimensions of the standard 0-6-0ST.

Table 2.2   0-6-0ST dimensions

Class	Wheel Diameter	Cylinders	Boiler Diameter	Length	Heating Surface	Tank Capacity	Weight
		inches			sq ft	gallons	
Old I	3ft 1$\frac{3}{8}$in	11 x 17	2ft 9in	7ft 3in	345	420	-
K	3ft 1$\frac{3}{8}$in	12 x 17	2ft 9in	7ft 9in	366	450	18tons10cwt
L	3ft 0in	12 x 18	3ft 1in	7ft 9in	448	450	-
M	3ft 0in	13 x 18	3ft 4in	8ft 4in	542	550	22tons10cwt
Q	3ft 6in	14 x 20	3ft 6in	8ft 8in	660	600	27tons 2cwt
O	3ft 9in	15 x 22	3ft 10in	8ft 6in	752	700	29tons13cwt

Figure 2.13 shows *Silverdale*, number 169 of 1865, an early M class, with many Wilson features visible, including a fluted safety-valve cover and rectangular number plate. The ornate cab, which is built onto the original spectacle plate, must be from a later date.

Figure 2.13 *Silverdale*, MW no. 169 of 1865.
(photograph R.C.Riley Collection.)

Figure 2.14 shows *Conduit* No.1, no. 244 of 1867, K class. In 1947 this engine moved to the National Coal Board, West Midlands Area, where she lasted until 1952.

Figure 2.14 *Conduit No.1*, MW no.244 of 1867.
(photograph J.M.Jarvis)

Figure 2.15 shows *Barrow Docks No.3*, another K class, no. 326 of 1870. All the early features are still visible, but a simple cab has evolved which remained a Manning Wardle feature on their small engines for many years.

Figure 2.15 *Barrow Docks No.3*, a K class MW no.326 of 1870.
(photograph R.C Riley Collection)

Figure 2.16 MW no.654 of 1875.
(photograph by the author)

The 0-6-0ST, MW no. 654 of 1875 in figure 2.16 had the usual varied history. She started with the name of *Alvechurch* at Ramshaw Colliery of the Chesterfield & Boythorpe Colliery Company. After returning to Manning Wardle, she went to the Greystone Lime Company at Oxted in 1921 where I took this photograph in 1935. In 1941 she went to the War Department.

Figure 2.17 *Conduit No 4,* MW no.1326 of 1896, class O.
(photograph by the author)

Figure 2.18 *Knowles*, class K, MW no.1520 of 1905, A.Knowles & Son Ltd, Pendleton Colliery, later Bridgewater Colliery Ltd, and then to Manchester Collieries Ltd. (photograph R.C.Riley Collection.)

Figure 2.19.*Mermaid*, MW no.1294 of 1894, class Q 0-6-0ST, working for contractors C.J.Willis. (photograph Dr.I.C.Allen)

Figure 2.20 *Aynho*, MW no.1722 of 1907, class L, looking very smart at the Conduit Colliery
where she arrived from contractors Walter Scott & Middleton.
(photograph by the author)

Figure 2.21 MW no.2046 of 1926, class M, 0-6-OST *Hendon*, working at the
Horton Asylum Railway. This was the last but one Manning Wardle locomotive built.
(photograph R.C.Riley)

0-8-0 Tank engine

Only three British-built eight-coupled steam locomotives saw industrial service in this country. One of these was built by Manning Wardle in 1914, works no.1853, for the Bridgewater Colliery.

A powerful engine was needed here to haul heavy loads up a 1 in 50 gradient, with steeper sections as severe as 1 in 28. This locomotive was not a complete success, as she suffered from poor steaming and a number of small defects. The very long original side tanks were later reduced in length.

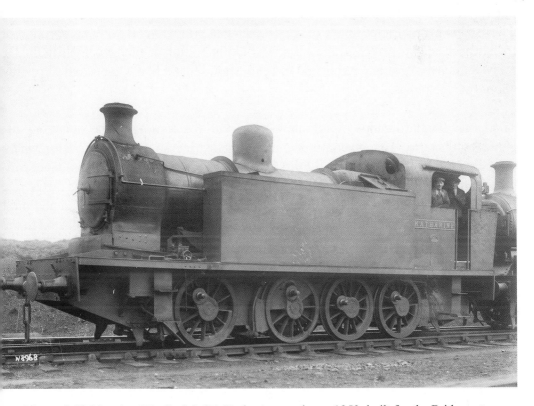

Figure 2.22 Manning Wardle 0-8-0T, *Katharine*, works no.1853, built for the Bridgewater Collieries in 1914. The photograph shows the reduced length of the side tanks.
(photograph National Railway Museum)

CHAPTER THREE

Narrow Gauge Railways

The standard gauge of railways, a little less than five feet, has a very ancient history. It mirrored the distance between the wheels of carts in Roman times and archaeological evidence shows that this hardly varied over 2000 years. A narrower gauge was used in the restricted space of dark mediaeval mine tunnels where some kind of track was needed for steering the carts. An old illustration of such a vehicle in the De Re Metallica of Agricola, published in 1556, shows that it had wheels that were only about two feet apart.

The larger standard gauge rapidly developed with the coming of the steam engine. However, the narrow gauge continued in mining districts such as North Wales, where the Festiniog Railway became the first narrow-gauge steam-driven passenger railway in Britain. Two of the smallest steam engines ever built were supplied by George England & Company for this railway in 1863. Manning Wardle designed and built two 0-4-2ST five years later for the Festiniog & Blaenau railway, an extension to the Festiniog Railway.

As the main railways developed rapidly in England, they produced a system of standard-gauge branch lines. This left little room for a subsidiary network of narrow-gauge lines that evolved in some parts of the continent; nevertheless some narrow-gauge passenger railways did appear in England during the 1870s. Manning Wardle built specially designed engines for most of these early lines and their industrial locomotives were used in many of them until the end.

Festiniog & Blaenau Railway

This railway, which operated from 1868 to 1883, was under four miles long and built as a feeder for the Festiniog Railway. It was planned to carry slate traffic and the quarrymen between Blaenau and Festiniog.

Two 0-4-2 saddle tank locomotives were ordered for the opening from Manning Wardle. These had works numbers 258 and 259 of 1868, and were the first this firm had designed for such a narrow gauge of 1ft 11 ins. They were narrower and taller than the corresponding tank engines on the Festiniog Railway (figure 3.1).

These two engines disappeared in 1883 and were sold to the Ruabon Coal and Coke Company, when the Great Western Railway built their branch line from Bala to Festiniog. The new standard gauge line was built along the old course of the narrow gauge railway.

Figure 3.1 MW no.259 of 1858, designed for the Festiniog and Blaenau Railway.
(from 'Engineering', 1870)

Ravenglass & Eskdale Railway

The first public narrow-gauge railway in England was the 3ft gauge Ravenglass & Eskdale which opened in 1875. This ran for nearly seven miles up into the mountains in the Lake District with mineral traffic as its main justification.

Manning Wardle built two small 0-6-0 tank engines for this line. The first was *Devon*, no. 545 of 1875, and this was followed by a second, slightly different engine *Nab Gill*, no. 629 of 1876.

Figure 3.2 MW no. 545 of 1875, *Devon* on the Ravenglass & Eskdale Railway.
(photograph National Railway Museum)

The ore traffic soon disappeared, but these engines continued for thirty years until the railway was closed, first to passengers in 1908 and then to goods on 30th April 1913. The railway was reopened in 1915 on the 15in gauge, and many interesting locomotives were built for this line and some are still running.

Figure 3.3 *Devon* hauling a train on the Ravenglass & Eskdale Railway.
(photograph National Railway Museum)

Southwold Railway

The 3ft gauge Southwold Railway was just under nine miles long and ran to the Suffolk town of Southwold on the east coast of England. The Railway opened in 1879 using three small 2-4-0 side-tank engines with very tall chimneys, built by Sharp Stewart.

The railway ran for fifty years and, in spite of some mocking postcards printed locally, it provided efficient transport from the coast at Southwold to the main railway system of the outside world.

In 1914 when the harbour branch was being built, an additional locomotive was needed and the much larger 0-6-2T No.4, *Wenhaston*, no. 1845 was ordered from Manning Wardle (figure 3.4). Painted in their standard dark green, with light and dark green lines, and black wheels lined in red, *Wenhaston* was much more powerful than the earlier locomotives, and was well liked by the footplate men. In the closing years of the railway she did a large share of the work. She was thoroughly overhauled in 1928 at Southwold and was given a brick arch supplied by Manning Wardle to reduce fuel consumption.

The line was closed in 1929, but the locomotives remained in the shed until the railway was dismantled twelve years later.

Figure 3.4 0-6-2T, *Wenhaston* No 4 MW no.1845 of 1915, of the 3ft gauge Southwold Railway. (photograph J.A.G.H.Coltas)

Lynton & Barnstaple Railway

The Lynton & Barnstaple Railway opened in 1898 from the main line at Barnstaple in Devonshire, nineteen miles to the coast at Lynton. This 1ft 11in railway was believed to have been modelled on the Festiniog Railway in Wales.

Manning Wardle supplied three impressive 2-6-2Ts, works numbers 1361 *Yeo*, 1362 *Exe* and 1363 *Taw*. They needed to be powerful to deal with the many 1 in 50 gradients in both directions, and were the biggest 2ft gauge locomotives ever to operate in Britain. After a first year's successful traffic, a fourth engine was required, and the Railway purchased the 2-4-2T *Lyn* from Baldwin in Philadelphia.

After the Grouping in 1923, the Lynton & Barnstaple Railway was taken over by the newly formed Southern Railway, which supported the little railway by placing an order in 1925 for another Manning Wardle 2-6-2T, *Lew*, no. 2042.

Figure 3.5 Two of the Lynton & Barnstaple 2-6-2Ts at Barnstaple. These are the first and the last supplied, MW no.1361 of 1897 *Yeo* and MW no.2042 of 1925 *Lew*.
(photograph National Railway Museum)

During the 1930s, the Southern Railway, which was spending money on electrification, discovered that the Lynton & Barnstaple section was not making a profit. When it was proposed to close the railway, it was noted that those who had made their way to Barnstaple to protest against its closure had all travelled there by road! In 1935, the railway was closed and the older locomotives were all cut up on the site. However, the most recent one, *Lew*, managed to escape to South America where she found work on a coffee plantation in Brazil.

Figure 3.6 MW no.1361 of 1897, *Yeo*, at the interchange platform at Barnstaple.
(photograph by the author)

Figure 3.7 MW no.2042 of 1925, *Lew*, at Barnstaple.
(photograph by the author)

Jersey Railways & Tramways

A railway was built in 1884 along part of the south coast of Jersey in the Channel Islands. Manning Wardle supplied two 3ft 6in gauge 2-4-0T's, *St. Heliers*, no. 916 and *St. Aubin*, no. 917. Both survived until the line closed in 1936.

Figure 3.8. MW no.916 of 1884, *St. Heliers*.
Official works photograph before delivery to the Jersey Railways.
(photograph National Railway Museum)

Kettering Ironstone Tramway

This 3ft gauge railway was a flourishing industrial line with three Manning Wardle locomotives and kept going until the late 1960s.

The Kettering Iron and Coal Company built a steadily lengthening tramway to carry iron ore to the smelting furnaces and connect with the main line railways. The line opened in 1879 with two Black Hawthorn locomotives, but later two more powerful Manning Wardle locomotives were purchased to cope with the gradients of the main line of the system. The other two smaller engines were relegated to shunting duties at the furnace end of the line. This had been continuously growing because, as each iron field became worked out, the railway had to be extended until it was eventually four miles long.

The Manning Wardle engines were: No 6, works no. 1123 of 1889, rebuilt by Stephenson & Hawthorn in 1949; No 7, works no. 1370 of 1897; and No 8, works no. 1675 of 1906. The last one of these three has been preserved.

Figure 3.9 *Kettering Furnaces No 7*, MW no.1370 of 1897.
(photograph R.C.Riley Collection)

Furzebrook Railway

This was a 2ft 8in gauge railway built by Pike Brothers & Co. Ltd. to serve their clay mines in Dorset. This railway was only three miles long but ran through delightful, partly wooded countryside to a trans-shipment point on the branch line at Furzebrook, between Wareham and Swanage.

Two Peckett locomotives worked here as well as two built by Manning Wardle. *Tertius*, (figure 3.10) no. 999 of 1886, 0-6-0ST, was rebuilt in 1911. When she was again rebuilt, locally in 1951, the available new boiler from the Lewin engine *Tiny* was found to be too wide to fit between the frames, and it had to be mounted in a very high position giving *Tertius* a rather top-heavy appearance. The other Manning Wardle locomotive was *Quintus*, 0-4-0ST no. 1854 of 1914 (figure 3.11).

The railway was closed in 1957.

Figure 3.10 *Tertius*, MW no.999 of 1888 seen at Furzebrook in 1935 before the second rebuilding. (photograph by the author)

B. Fayle & Company, Corfe

Also in Dorset, on a line connected with the Furzebrook Railway, was another narrow gauge Manning Wardle locomotive. This was 3ft 6in gauge 0-4-0ST *Thames*, number 1552 of 1902, which started life at Becton Sewage Works. After being re-gauged to 3ft 9in she eventually reached B.Fayle's line near Corfe Castle where I photographed her in 1935.

Figure 3.11 MW no.1854 of 1914, *Quintus* at Furzebrook.
(photograph by the author)

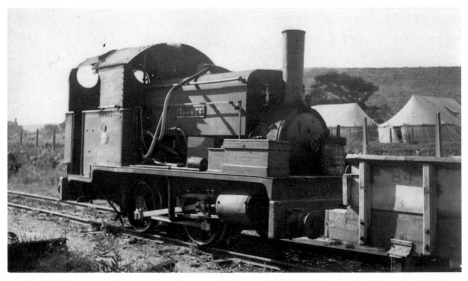

Figure 3.12 MW no.1552 of 1902, 0-4-0ST, *Thames* on B. Fayle's line near Corfe Castle, Dorset.
(photograph by the author)

CHAPTER FOUR

Standard Gauge Light Railways

Right back to the 1860s and 1870s Manning Wardle had built locomotives for minor railways. Whilst these were mostly 2-4-0T types, built for light passenger trains on branch lines, they also built some unusual locomotives, such as the unique 2-6-0T for the Garstang & Knott End Railway.

As late as the 1930s there were still some small standard gauge railways unaffected by the grouping of 1923, and more than half of these lines had at least one product of Manning Wardle. Some of these, as might be expected, were small 0-4-0 and 0-6-0 saddle tank engines, but there were also a few other types still in use.

Cleobury Mortimer and Ditton Priors Railway

The Cleobury Mortimer and Ditton Priors Light Railway in Shropshire was opened for goods and passengers in 1908. It was twelve miles long and was mostly concerned with the stone traffic from the Abdon Clee Stone Company at Ditton Priors. When the railway opened, Manning Wardle supplied two heavy outside cylinder 0-6-0 saddle tank locomotives, numbers 1734 and 1735 of 1908. They had brass name plates of *Burwarton* and *Cleobury* (figure 4.1).

After the main line grouping in 1923, these engines became Great Western Railway No.28 (*Cleobury*) and No.29 (*Burwarton*) and were later rebuilt at Swindon as pannier tanks (Figure 4.2).

Although the railway was closed to passengers in 1938, both engines survived until the days of British Rail and then were scrapped in 1953.

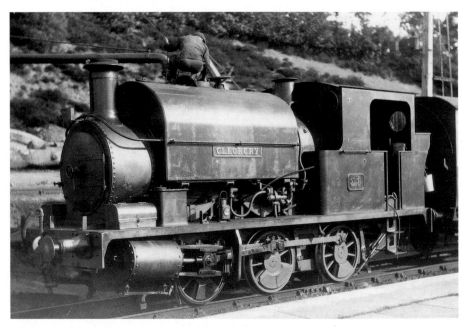

Figure 4.1 *Cleobury,* 0-6-0ST, MW no.1735 of 1908, on the Cleobury Mortimer and Ditton Priors Railway. In 1923 she became Great Western Railway. No.28.
(photograph R.C.Riley)

Figure 4.2 No.29 *Burwarton*, 0-6-0PT, MW no.1734 of 1908 on the Cleobury Mortimer and Ditton Priors Railway. Rebuilt as a pannier tank by the Great Western Railway.
(photograph W.A.Carnwell)

Edge Hill Light Railway

The Edge Hill Light Railway in Warwickshire, which included in its locomotive stock a Manning Wardle 0-4-0 saddle tank, had quite an extraordinary history.

The railway was opened in 1919, but only three-and-a-half miles were ever completed. After a level section, over which the railway was authorised to carry passengers, there was an incline of 1 in 8 to reach the level of the iron stone mines that the line was designed to serve.

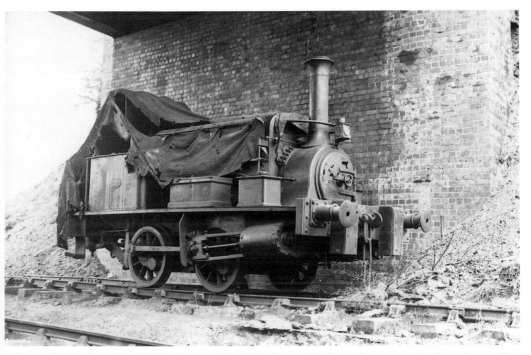

Figure 4.3 *Sankey*, 0-4-0ST, MW no.1088 of 1888, class F. Formerly a contractor's engine on the Manchester Ship Canal she joined the Edge Hill Light Railway in 1924. After the railway was abandoned in 1925 she stood under the road bridge for the next 20 years.
(photograph by the author)

Two ex-Brighton Terrier 0-6-0Ts served the lower part of the line below the cable-worked incline by which the railway was raised three hundred feet to the level of the ironstone workings. The locomotive on the higher section, obtained in 1922 when the incline had been completed, was *Sankey*, a Manning Wardle 0-4-0ST, no.1088 of 1888, class F. Originally working as a contractor's engine on the Manchester Ship

Canal, she had a varied career before reaching Edge Hill. *Sankey* was able to ascend the incline under her own power, assisted by cable with two wagons as counter-weight.

By 1924 the iron ore trade had declined and the last load came down the incline in January 1925. At this point the railway just stopped. The big steam excavator was left with its jib ready for the next scoop, and the two Terriers stood with their trains nearby. *Sankey* was left at the top of the incline underneath the road bridge which served as her shed (figure 4.3). The railway remained in this state of suspended animation for nearly twenty years until the locomotives were finally cut up in 1946. When I visited the railway in 1932, I was reminded of the *Marie Celeste* mystery in which a sailing ship was found in the ocean, all sails set, with even the meals set out for the crew of whom no trace was ever found.

Figure 4.4 *Knott End*, 0-6-0T, MW no.1732 of 1908.
(photograph National Railway Museum)

Garstang and Knott End Railway

This railway was opened in 1870 to join Garstang on the West Coast main line to

Knott End, eleven miles distant on the coast north of Fleetwood.

In 1874 a small Manning Wardle 0-4-0-ST was purchased from A.Pilling, the contractors of the Lancaster Union Railway at Boston, Lincolnshire. This engine, *Union*, no.226 of 1868, proved to be too small for the trains over the railway's main route and was replaced by a larger Hudswell Clarke 0-6-0ST, the first of three similar locomotives.

The newly incorporated Knott End Railway purchased two new locomotives from Manning Wardle in 1908. The first was *Knott End*, no.1732 of 1908, a handsome 0-6-0 side tank with outside cylinders (figure 4.4).

A most unusual locomotive followed in 1909, works no.1747, *Blackpool*. This was a 2-6-0T, one of the few ever built to this wheel arrangement, and is shown in her original condition in figure 4.5. Both these engines survived the grouping in 1923, becoming LMS no.11302 and no.11680.

Figure 4.5 *Blackpool*, 2-6-0T, MW no.1747 of 1909.
This survived the grouping to become LMS No.11680.
(photograph National Railway Museum)

Hundred of Manhood and Selsey Tramway

This was under the control of Colonel Stephens, who also managed thirteen other minor railways and seems to have had a particular liking for second-hand Manning Wardle locomotives. The line was opened in 1897 and ran from Chichester to the coastal resort of Selsey, a distance of seven miles. It operated for twenty-seven years without any proper legal authority, and in 1924 the name was changed to the West Sussex Railway.

The only locomotive that was built new for the line was a 2-4-2T from Pecketts. The first Manning Wardle to reach the railway was no.21 of 1861, *Sidlesham* (old I class). Originally named *Henrietta*, she worked as a colliery locomotive for J.&J. Charlesworth of Rothwell and later for Meakin and Dean of Birkenhead. Further contractor's work at Blagdon led to an overhaul by Hawthorn Leslie who sold her to Colonel Stephens in 1907 (figure 4.6).

Figure 4.6 *Sidlesham*, MW no.21 of 1861, old I class, of the Selsey Tramway, crossing the lifting bridge over the canal. She was bought for the tramway in 1907. (photograph Chichester District Museum)

No.4, *Morous*, Manning Wardle no.178 of 1866, was also an old class I and had a long career before reaching the Selsey Tramway (figure 4.7). She was built to the order of Mr T.R. Crampton, contractor of Fenny Compton, and bore the name *Crampton* when new. In 1871 she was purchased after working on the construction of the newly opened East and West Junction Railway and named *Kineton*. After rebuilding in 1900, *Morous* was first acquired by Colonel Stephens for the Shropshire and Montgomery Railway and was transferred to Selsey in 1924.

Figure 4.7 No.4, *Morous,* 0-6-0ST, MW no.178 of 1866 of the Selsey Tramway.
(photograph S.W.Baker)

The third Manning Wardle engine was *Ringing Rock*, a K class, no.890 of 1883 and had a series of jobs and names from four successive industrial concerns. Originally named *Vida* at J.C.Billups, contractors of Cardiff, then as *No.7* at Pauling & Company, she went to the Royal Ordnance Department in 1915. After the war she became *Wembley* with McAlpines until in 1922 she joined the West Sussex Railway, and had a new right hand cylinder in 1923.

Figure 4.8 *Ringing Rock*, 0-6-0ST, MW no.890 of 1883, K class, of the Selsey Tramway.
(photograph by the author)

Colonel Stephens transferred the name *Ringing Rock* to number 890 from another Manning Wardle engine, number 630 of the Kent and East Sussex Railway (page 51) which then became *Hesperus*. Most of the original design features of the K class can still be seen in my photograph of this locomotive, taken at Chichester in 1934 (figure 4.8).

The railway provided a useful service to local people for many years, but fell on hard times in the 1920s with the spread of the local bus services. Final closure was in January 1935, when the last train ran from Selsey to Chichester. Both *Morous* and *Ringing Rock* lasted to the end.

Kent & East Sussex Railway

Originally named the Rother Valley Railway, this was Colonel Stephen's fourth venture. It had many interesting locomotives including two ex-Brighton Terriers, but only one Manning Wardle, no.630 of 1876.

This locomotive of the altered Q class started with the name *Ringing Rock* on the North Pembroke and Fishguard Railway. In 1898 she joined the Great Western Railway, became no.1380 and was rebuilt at Swindon in 1902. Then in 1914, after a short period with the Bute Works Supply Company, she was sold to the Kent & East Sussex Railway and renamed *Hesperus* (figure 4.9). She was scrapped in 1941.

A preservation society was formed and the Kent & East Sussex Railway was opened in 1974. Preserved Manning Wardle engines have run on this line.

Figure 4.9 *Hesperus,* 0-6-0ST, MW no.630 of 1876 of the Kent & East Sussex Railway
After joining the Great Western Railway, she was rebuilt at Swindon,
bought by the KESR in 1914 and renamed *Hesperus.*
(photograph Locomotive Publishing Company)

Lee-on-Solent Railway

This railway connected Lee-on-Solent on the south coast with the LSWR at For
Brockhurst, being one of the first railways constructed under the Light Railway Order of 1864.

Their first locomotive was a 2-4-0T by George England and was on public display in
the Great Exhibition of 1862. The second was a Manning Wardle purchased second-
hand from Waterloo Main Colliery. It was then purchased by the LSWR for contractor's work at Okehampton. This was Manning Wardle no.50 of 1852, an old class I
and shown in figure 4.10 working a train at Fort Brockhurst. At one time given the
name *Lady Portsmouth*, this engine was No.392 in the running department of the
LSWR.

This was one of the last engines at work with the very ancient type of fluted cast-iron
safety valve cover. The LSWR sold the engine in 1913, and she survived under
different ownerships under the name of *Hecate* until 1929.

Figure 4.10 MW no.50 of 1862, 0-6-0ST, at Fort Brockhurst on the Lee-on-Solent Railway.
(photograph Locomotive Publishing Company)

Millwall Extension Railway

In 1880 Manning Wardle were awarded a contract to build three small standard gauge locomotives to a special design to limit the weight over the bridges on the Millwall Extension Railway. These were 2-4-0 side tank engines, numbers 749, 750, 776, and at the time they were the smallest locomotives in regular passenger service on the standard gauge in Britain. Numbered 3, 4, and 6, at one time they had advertisements mounted on their side tanks. One of these locomotives, No.6, is illustrated in figure 4.11.

Figure 4.11 *No.6*, 2-4-0T, MW no.776 of 1880 of the Millwall Extension Railway, one of three engines which worked on this branch line until 1929.
(photograph National Railway Museum)

For many years heavy traffic ran on this railway due to the connection with Millwall Football Club. By 1922 the three engines were worn out and were replaced by three ex-GWR rail motors. However, these were not satisfactory and the three Manning Wardle engines were returned to service. The line was closed in 1926 because of the General Strike.

North Sunderland Railway

This railway was opened in 1898 running for four miles from Chathill on the main line to Seahouses on the coast of Sunderland. It was operated with one locomotive, Manning Wardle 0-6-0ST *Bamburgh*, and three coaching vehicles (figure 4.12). Rebuilt in 1920, it was sold for scrap in 1949, two years before the railway was closed.

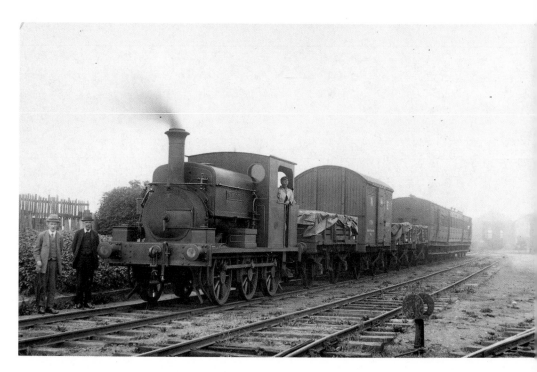

Figure 4.12 *Bamburgh*, 0-6-0ST, MW no.1394 of 1898 on the North Sunderland Railway. (photograph J.K.Williams Collection)

Oxford and Aylesbury Tramroad

This started in 1871 as the Wotton Tramway, the private goods railway of the Duke of Buckingham, using a geared Aveling & Porter locomotive. In 1888 the line had been extended to Brill and a passenger service operated from Quainton Road.

The first of three Manning Wardle engines was a K type, no.616 of 1876, as shown in figure 4.13 heading a passenger train at Quainton Road. It had been delivered new to T.J. Waller, contractor of Manchester, and given the name *Prestwich*. After several more owners, during which the name *Huddersfield* was painted on the side of the tank, it joined the Tramroad about 1894. At one time the first section of the connecting rods were removed and *Huddersfield* worked as a 2-4-0ST. In view of the nature of the Brill Branch this may have served to reduce derailments. The name was later changed to *Wotton No.1*.

Figure 4.13 *Wotton No.1*, 0-6-0ST, MW no.616 of 1876, K class,
of the Oxford & Aylesbury Tramroad at Quainton Road.
(photograph Locomotive Publishing Company)

The next Manning Wardle locomotive that joined the line, no.1249 of 1894, another K class, arrived brand new. She was given the name *Earle Temple* in honour of the man who purchased the engine and rented her to the Company. The name was later changed to *Brill No.1*.

The third (K class) Manning Wardle locomotive was delivered in 1899, no.1415 and named *Wotton No.2*. The first *Wotton* was a Bagnall engine of Wotton Tramway days and was sold on the arrival of *Huddersfield*.

After the take-over by the Metropolitan Railway, the Manning Wardles continued their haulage work until they were eventually replaced by Beyer Peacock 4-4-0T engines that operated until the railway closed in 1935.

Weston, Clevedon and Portishead Railway

The Weston, Clevedon and Portishead Railway opened in 1897 between the two coastal towns of Weston and Clevedon in Somerset, finally reaching Portishead in 1907. In 1909 Colonel Stephens became the manager, and his fondness for Brighton Terriers and Manning Wardle locomotives was soon evident.

The railway had three Manning Wardle engines, the first was no.1135 of 1890. After arrival fourth-hand she was named No.2 *Portishead* and is shown in figure 4.14. In 1926 she was sold to local contractors Cowlin of Bristol but continued to work at Portishead. Her place was taken by the new No.2, a Brighton Terrier.

The next Manning Wardle purchased by Colonel Stephens was no.731 of 1881, an altered L class. This had a complicated history which included arriving at the Avonside Engine Company from the Barry Port & Gwendraeth Valley Railway as part-payment for another engine. After being rebuilt by Avonside, she arrived at Clevedon in 1904 and was named No.3 *Weston* (figure 4.15). She continued to run until the railway was closed in 1940.

The third Manning Wardle engine on this railway was works number 1970 of 1919. She was originally named *Hecate* and as *No.5* did most of the work during the railway's final years. Figure 4.16 shows the unusual form of the driving wheels.

Figure 4.14 No.2 *Portishead*, MW no.1134 of 1890, of the Weston, Clevedon and Portishead Railway. This was sold in 1920 and replaced by a Terrier. (photograph Locomotive Publishing Company)

Figure 4.15 *Weston*, MW no.731 of 1881 of the Weston, Clevedon and Portishead Railway. (photograph Locomotive Publishing Company)

Figure 4.16 MW no.1970 of 1919 of the Weston, Clevedon and Portishead Railway. The cast-iron driving wheels and the stove-pipe chimney were both wartime features. (photograph by the author)

Figure 4.17 Weston, Clevedon and Portishead Railway, *No.5* crossing the Triangle in the centre of Clevedon. Note the uniformed official carrying a red flag. (photograph J.G.Dewing)

The Wantage Tramway

This opened as a horse tramway and ran for two miles along public roads from Wantage to the Great Western Railway station at Wantage Road.

Although the tramway opened with horses as the motive power, after a short time a steam tram-car started to operate. A fine series of tram-engines and trailers appeared on this line. Later a 0-4-0 well tank, *Shannon*, built in 1857 by George England, joined the tramway. Usually known as *Jane*, she operated until the line closed and was later preserved and put into working order.

No.7 *Massey*, 0-4-0ST, Manning Wardle no.1057 of 1888, arrived at Wantage in 1893 (figure 4.18) having worked on the Manchester Ship Canal during its construction. There were one hundred other Manning Wardle engines working there including sister engine *Sankey* of the ill-fated Edge Hill Light Railway (page 45).

Figure 4.18 Wantage Tramway, MW no.1057 of 1888, hauling Tram No.4 about 1914.
(photograph Chapman & Son, Dawlish)

Another Manning Wardle was purchased in 1919, but had a much less happy career. This was number 515 of 1875, H class, and was bought second-hand from Woolwich Arsenal where she was originally named *The Gunner* and later *The Driver*. Unfortunately, although this engine could raise steam quickly, she could never maintain working pressure and as a result was hardly ever used. When broken up at Wantage a year later, the trouble was diagnosed as a broken steam pipe that had leaked steam directly to the smoke-box without any reaching the cylinders.

The other Manning Wardle, No.7 (she never carried a name, although she was known to the engine-men as *Mary*), continued to show herself as the most successful engine owned by the Tramway. I photographed her at Wantage in 1935 (figure 4.19) and she lasted until the line's demise in 1946. After working on the demolition of the Tramway, she moved on to start another career with A.Adams of Newport, Monmouth.

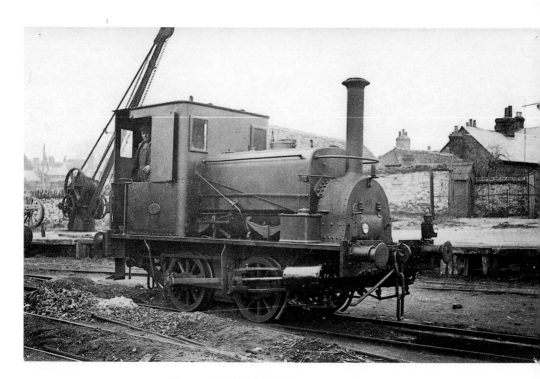

Figure 4.19 0-4-0ST,MW no.1057 of 1888.
This was *Wantage Tramway No.7*, known to the engine men as *Mary*.
(photograph by the author)

CHAPTER FIVE

Main Line Locomotives

Manning Wardle did not build main line express locomotives although many contractors' engines found their way to the main line companies. However, a few very successful special designs were built for lines that eventually found themselves in the big four formed in the grouping of 1923. These four were the Great Western, the London, Midland & Scottish, the London & North Eastern, and the Southern Railway. Manning Wardle locomotives were supplied to several sub-groups of these railways before the 1923 grouping.

Great Western Railway

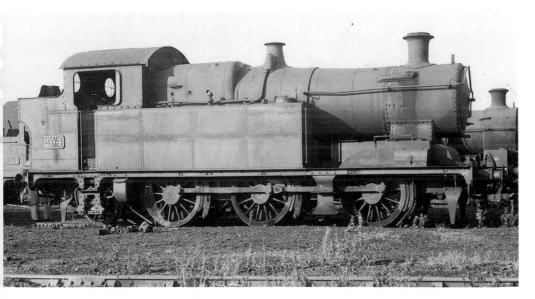

Figure 5.1 One of the main line 0-6-2T built for the Taff Vale Railway,
MW no.1704 of 1907 that started life as TVR No.94 and was rebuilt at Swindon.
(photograph C.F.H.Oldham, R.C.Riley Collection)

The Taff Vale Railway has a history that goes back to 1836 when it opened between Merthyr Tydfil and Cardiff. When the railway was absorbed by the Great Western in 1921 there were two hundred and seventy-five locomotives and one hundred and twelve miles of track.

Manning Wardle supplied seven 0-6-2T in 1907 to the Taff Vale Railway, works numbers 1698-1704. Some of them lasted until the days of British Railway before being scrapped in the early 1950s.

London Midland & Scottish Railway

The Midland Railway was an important member of this group and a very early Manning Wardle locomotive reached this line in 1870. This was 0-6-0WT, *Rutland*, no. 12 of 1860, originally sold to Dunston & Barlow. She was later transferred to the Sheepbridge Iron Company, finally arriving at the Midland Railway in 1870 where she was re-numbered 1064 and later 2064 (figure 5.2). She continued to work on the Midland Railway until she was withdrawn in 1900.

Figure 5.2 MW no.12 of 1860, *Rutland*, as Midland Railway No.2064.
(Photograph R.C.Riley Collection)

London & North Eastern Railway

The Great Eastern Railway was composed of several small lines, and one of these was the Thetford and Watton Railway. Two fine Manning Wardle 2-4-0T no.298 and 299 of 1870 were sold to this railway where they were numbered 1 and 2. The Great Eastern Railway re-numbered the two engines 802 and 803, and they continued to run until 1888.

Figure 5.3 MW no.299 of 1870, sold to W.P.Birch, of the Thetford and Watton Railway. This locomotive later became Great Eastern Railway No.803.
(photograph National Railway Museum)

Great North of Scotland Railway

In 1914 two very successful 0-4-2T locomotives of the Z4 class were designed and built by Manning Wardle, no.1858 and no.1859. They were followed in 1915 by two slightly different Z3 class engines, no.1884 and no.1885. The latter one became British Rail No.68192 (figure 5.4). These engines had a long and useful life, mostly around the docks in Aberdeen, and finally disappeared between 1956 and 1960.

Figure 5.4. MW 0-4-2T, British Rail No.68192, of the former Great North of Scotland Railway. (photograph Brian Morrison)

Southern Railway

The London & South Western Railway possessed at one time as many as six Manning Wardle saddle tank engines. Three of these were 0-4-0ST and were all purchased from R.T.Relf, contractors of Okehampton. The first was no.594 of 1876 *Pioneer*, and was bought from Relf in 1881 for shunting at Plymouth. As LSWR No.407 she had a varied career, working underground in the early days of the Waterloo and City railway until replaced by an electric locomotive. She worked as a tipping engine on the widening of the Woking to Basingstoke line, and was also hired out to the Portsea Gas Light Company and later to Bournemouth Corporation. In 1906, No.0407, as she was then, was renamed *Reno*. She was withdrawn from service in 1919 and was finally scrapped in 1921.

Figure 5.5 MW no.594 of 1876, LSWR No.407 seen at Poole in 1902.
(photograph C.H Eden, R.C.Riley Collection)

Two other sister engines were no.628 of 1876, *Jessie*, which later became LSWR No.408 and was stationed at Plymouth; and no.379 of 1872, *Lydford*, which was sold to R.T.Relf, contractors on the Devon & Cornwall Railway. In 1883 she worked at Okehampton where she became LSWR No.457, *St. Michael*.

Of the three 0-6-0ST, the first was no.50 of 1862, *Lady Portsmouth*. As LSWR No.392 she was lent to the Lee-on-Solent Railway as described in chapter 4.

Jumbo and *Sambo* were Manning Wardle K class 0-6-0ST, bought from the contractors J.T.Chappell and were numbered 458 and 459 by the LSWR. *Jumbo*, no.709 of 1879, was painted Brighton yellow when she arrived and re-named *Steyning*, and she worked for ten years on the Bodmin and Wadebridge line. The history of *Sambo* is rather more obscure.

The South Eastern and Chatham Railway had two Manning Wardle locomotives. The first was no.767 of 1881 and became SECR No.313. After the grouping in 1923 she was re-numbered by the Southern as No.225S in the service list and spent many years working at the Meldon Quarry near Okehampton, where most of the track ballast for the railway was extracted. She was withdrawn in 1938.

The SECR also purchased a Q class 0-6-0ST, no.1154 of 1890. This engine spent most of her life as a shunter at Ashford Works. She was still active when the SECR became part of the Southern Railway, apparently in much the original condition, except for the stove-pipe chimney. She lasted until 1932.

Figure 5.6 MW no.767 of 1881 as Southern No.225S at Meldon Quarry.
(photograph H.C.Casserley)

Figure 5.7 MW no.1154 of 1890, No.353 of the South Eastern & Chatham Railway.
(photograph Locomotive Publishing Company)

The London Brighton and South Coast Railway purchased two 0-6-0 'ballast engines' from Manning Wardle in 1866. These were numbers 185 and 186 and were numbered LBSCR 219 and 220 respectively. They proved to be very successful engines.

After nearly twenty years No.219 was sold to the West Lancashire Railway where it was re-numbered 5 and named *Brighton*. No.220 had the fluted dome and safety valve cover replaced with a conventional type by Mr. Stroudley and lasted until 1887.

Figure 5.8. MW no.186 of 1866, numbered 220 by the LBSCR,
where she was used on main line goods trains.
(drawing from Locomotive Magazine)

The Freshwater, Yarmouth & Newport Railway on the Isle of Wight also joined the Southern Railway in 1923. In 1913 this railway purchased two engines, one of which was Manning Wardle 0-6-0ST, works no.1555 of 1902, class Q (the other one was a second-hand Brighton Terrier). Originally named *Northolt* she became No.56 at the contractors Pauling & Company, but was re-numbered No.1 and re-named *Medina* by the Southern Railway.

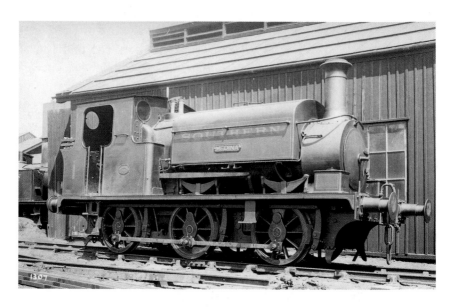

Figure 5.9 No.1 *Medina*, MW no.1555 of 1902, of the Freshwater, Yarmouth & Newport Railway. (photograph Locomotive Publishing Company)

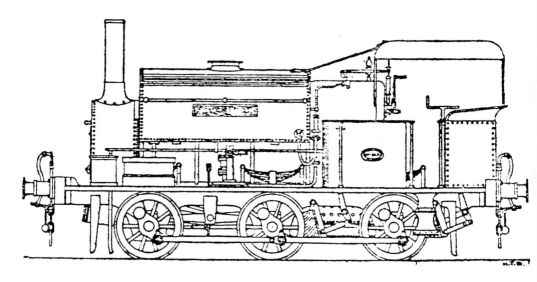

Figure 5.10 0-6-0ST, *Bembridge*, MW no.517 of 1875, class M, of the Isle of Wight Railway. (drawing from Locomotive Magazine).

After the grouping in 1923, both the Freshwater engines were retained in service. No.1, which was the most modern engine on the Island, proved very useful as a shunting engine at Medina Wharf, while the Terrier hauled trains on the branch line. *Medina* was scrapped in 1932.

The Isle of Wight Railway had one Manning Wardle class M 0-6-0ST, no.517 of 1875. This engine belonged to Scott & Edwards, the contractor making the Brading Harbour branch, and was named *Stanley*. She was taken over in 1882 when the IWR started to work the branch and, re-named *Bembridge*, was used almost entirely on this line. About 1910 some alterations were made which included the fitting of a stove-pipe chimney, and in 1917 she was bought by the Government for war service in Iraq, but never returned.

CHAPTER SIX

Unconventional Locomotives

Like most of the smaller builders, Manning Wardle at their Boyne Engine Works were usually full of industrial and contractor locomotives under construction or repair. Nevertheless, they were always prepared to undertake construction of unconventional designs. These included tram engines or rail car units, crane engines, and even petrol engines or armoured train locomotives.

Patent locomotives of J.B. Fell

One particular series of engines that Manning Wardle built was from the designs and inventions of the engineer John Barraclough Fell. In 1863 J.B.Fell patented his central rail system for any steep gradients having sharp curves, and for which he became justly famous. In this system, horizontal wheels were pressed against a central rail by a combination of levers and bevel wheels, and examples are still in operation to this day. Experiments were carried out on the steep gradients of the Cromford and High Peak Railway in Derbyshire, and the system was later used on the Mont Cenis Railway in Switzerland.

Manning Wardle built four of this type of Fell engines in 1872 for the Cantagallo Railway in Brazil, works numbers 376-9, one of which is shown in figure 6.1. This engine, later named *Disco T Macedo*, had four cylinders, two of which drove four coupled wheels that gripped the central rail. The outer cylinders drove the outside wheels in the usual way.The Centre Rail System made Fell famous, but he made several other worthwhile inventions, and Manning Wardle played an important part in two. One of these was the Aldershot Railway, built for the War Office in

1872 to Fell's design, for which Manning Wardle built *Ariel*, works no. 412, a 0-6-0 tender engine. This evolved from Fell's earlier 'monorail railway' in which the locomotive ran on a monorail supported on trestles, with an additional guide rail on each side.

The Aldershot Railway has been described as a 'gantry' rather than a monorail. The trains ran on two rails, only eighteen inches apart, supported on elevated trestles that were three feet apart and carried two lower guide rails. The simple diagram in figure 6.2 shows the principle of the support and guide rails. The train ran steadily on the Aldershot Railway, up to a speed of thirty miles per hour, but further tests, such as erecting and dismantling the track, were continually required by the authorities.

Figure 6.1 MW no. 377 of 1872. Fell's Central Rail locomotive
for the Cantagallo Railway in Brazil.
(Photograph National Railway Museum)

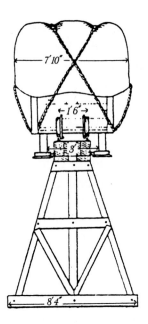

Figure 6.2 The 'gantry' system as used in the Fell patent Aldershot Railway. A bulky load is carried on the elevated 18in gauge rails and is supported by the guide rails which are 3ft apart.

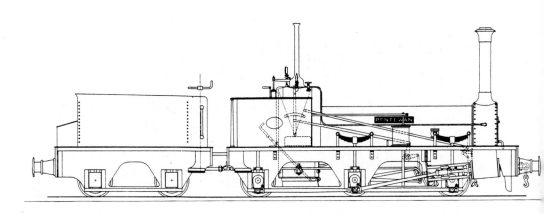

Figure 6.3 Fell's patent engine for the Pentewan Railway, MW no. 461 of 1873. This was a 2ft. 6in narrow gauge railway and no longer used guide rails.

After the demise of the Aldershot Railway, the next engines built by Manning Wardle to Fell's patent design were on the 2ft 6in gauge Pentewan Railway in Cornwall, which now discarded the guide rail altogether. Figure 6.3 shows the first of these engines, 0-6-0, *Pentewan*, no. 461 of 1873. This ran successfully for many years and was eventually replaced in 1886 by a similar engine, no. 994, *Trewithen*.

Crane Engines

A crane engine is a normal design of steam locomotive but carrying a crane jib mounted as an accessory. The earliest purpose-built crane locomotive was made by Dubs at the Glasgow Locomotive works in 1868 for use in their yard. By 1880 this firm had evolved a standard design with the crane portion built as a structure attached directly to the main frame at a point between the axles.

Figure 6.4 The first crane locomotive built by Manning Wardle,
a standard gauge 0-4-0T, works no. 578, built in 1875.
(photograph National Railway Museum)

Manning Wardle entered this field at an early date with a crane locomotive of similar general appearance This was no.578 of 1875, a 0-4-0 side tank engine built for the Kirkstall Forge in Leeds. It is believed that the crane structure had been removed before 1884 when the engine was sold to Hudswell Clarke.

Only four crane engines were ever built by Manning Wardle, and it was twenty-eight years before the second one left the Boyne Engine Works. It was a massive 0-6-0T, no. 1612 of 1903 built on the 5ft 6in gauge for the Secretary of State for India. This was the most successful of the four crane engines and was still operating in 1980, one of the last still in commercial use in the world.

Ten years later, the third engine followed, works no. 1811 of 1913, on the 3ft 6in gauge for the Victoria Falls and Transvaal Power Company. This locomotive only carried its crane for a short time, as it was removed by November 1914.

Figure 6.5 0-4-0T, MW crane locomotive, no. 1811 of 1913,
built on 3ft 6in gauge for the Victoria Falls and Transvaal Power Company.
(photograph the Hunslet Engine Company)

The final crane engine was built in 1918, works no. 1931, for Thomas Firth & Son of the Norfolk Steel Works, Sheffield, and was named *Noe*, No. 12. All these locomotives had their crane structure and auxiliary engines built at the works of Joseph Booth and Brothers of Rodley, Leeds.

Steam Tramways

The steam tram engine was a small 0-4-0 that hauled a single trailer, often a heavy double-decker, with a roof to protect the passengers from soot and smoke. Regulations demanded that 'the machinery must be concealed from view at all points above four inches from the level of the tracks'. Manning Wardle were pioneers in building tram locomotives and were involved in one of the first experimental steam-powered tramways at Ryde, on the Isle of Wight. They built 0-4-0ST, *Vectis*, no. 111 of 1864, for the Ryde Pier Commission who laid a tramway along the three-quarters of a mile Ryde Pier that connected with the Isle of Wight Railway.

On 14th March 1864, *Vectis*, under Mr.Wardle's personal supervision, was set to work on Ryde Pier. Unfortunately, in the first few days, the vibrations of the Pier were so great that the operation had to be postponed. After five months the tramway was opened, at first by horses and then, from 1881 to 1884, by steam until the line was later electrified.

Vectis soon found other work with the Northfleet Coal and Ballast Company, and Manning Wardle's next venture in this field was to supply two saddle tank locomotives to the 4ft gauge Pernambuco tramways in Brazil in 1866, no. 208 and 209. The entire machine was enclosed in a cab, a cowcatcher was fitted, and the exhaust was at one time condensed in the saddle tank. These were successful and six others followed in 1870.

Three of 'Fidlers Patent Steam Omnibus' type engines were exported to Buenos Aires in 1870. They were used on the 5ft 6in gauge with an articulated coach at each end of the locomotive, and the whole was over fifty feet long. These were no. 295 *La Plata*, no. 296 *Paraguay*, and no. 297 *Uruguay*.

Later more conventional tram engines were built for the home market for two large tramway systems in the Midlands. Between 1880 and 1882 six engines were built on the 4ft gauge for the North Staffordshire Tramways at Stoke, followed in 1885 by three standard gauge engines, no. 52, 53, and 54 for the Manchester, Bury, Rochdale and Oldham Tramways, one of which is illustrated in figure 6.6.

The first steam trams began to run in Britain in 1877, but only enjoyed a very short life-span before they were replaced by the new electric trams from about 1900.

Figure 6.6 MW no. 851 of 1885, 0-4-0 tram engine No. 83,of the Manchester, Bury, Rochdale and Oldham Tramways,at Hathershaw in 1895,with a double deck trailer. (photograph H.A.Whitcombe Collection)

Rail cars

After the turn of the century, many railway companies were faced with the growing problem of how to deal with uneconomical branch line traffic. What was later to be referred to as 'Inter City' travel as well as the local traffic on the extensive suburban Networks, had differing requirements from the services that could be satisfied by an occasional single carriage.

The first genuine 'rail car' designed to solve the problem was introduced by Dugald Drummond of the London and South Western Railway. His first design had a steam power unit built into the carriage, but this was found to have insufficient power. It later developed into a more powerful form where the 'works' were visible, sometimes leading to a separate small locomotive. Manning Wardle built this intermediate type for three different railways.

The first of five was built in 1906 for the Taff Vale Railway. Manning Wardle built the steam engine unit, no. 1676, and Brush Electrical produced the passenger portion.

Figure 6.7 Taff Vale rail car. Manning Wardle built the steam engine unit in 1906.
(photograph National Railway Museum)

Manning Wardle next built the power units for four cars for the Great Northern Railway of Ireland, numbers 1684-7. Two units were also built for the Dublin, Wicklow & Wexford Railway (figure 6.8), numbers 1692 and 1693. Later these two engines were separated and ran as 0-4-0T, *Imp* and *Elf*.

Figure 6.8 Rail car built for the Dublin, Wicklow & Wexford Railway.
The engine, MW no. 1693 of 1906, was later separated and ran as a 0-4-0T locomotive.
(photograph R.C.Riley Collection).

Armoured trains

In 1882 the Royal Engineers started to build up a unit to develop the military use of railways. With the campaign in Egypt in mind, they placed an order with the Secretary of State for War for four Manning Wardle saddle-tank engines.

These were two 0-4-0ST, numbers 792 and 826 of 1882, followed by two 0-6-0ST, K class, numbers 831 and 832. Later in the year, two of the engines reached Cairo and two also reached Ismailia. They hauled an 'iron-clad' train, which seems to have been the first iron-plated train armed with guns. Eventually it was handed over to the Navy at Alexandria.

The next armoured train powered by a Manning Wardle engine ran in the south of England. This was the Brighton Armoured Train. and it was hauled on its inaugural run by a LBSC 0-6-2T. A correspondent from The Times had reservations about the success of this venture, and he pointed out the ease with which a railway could be dynamited. The result was that the conservative military continued to show its devotion to the horse.

The Brighton Armoured Train in figure 6.9 had plating around the top of the two carriages to protect riflemen lying on the roof.

Figure 6.9 The Brighton Armoured Train on the beach at Newhaven in the 1890s.
The locomotive is 0-6-0ST *Bradford*, MW no. 403 of 1872, M class,
owned by the Newhaven Harbour Company
(photograph National Army Museum)

CHAPTER SEVEN

Locomotives Sold Abroad

Over two thousand steam locomotives were built by Manning Wardle, of which nearly four hundred were sold to foreign countries.

Heading the list of exports were South American countries. In Argentina, Chile, Brazil and Peru, the railways had mostly been planned and built by British engineers. Even after the railways had been taken over by the State, the British often retained a controlling interest.

As might be expected, India had a large number of Manning Wardle imports. Indian railways can be divided into broad and narrow gauge, and most of the company's engines were in the lighter metre-gauge group. At least one of the latter, an 0-6-2T, was still operating as late as 1986.

Of the forty-four exported to Russia, about half were built for the 5ft gauge, the rest were 3ft 6in or 3ft gauge. Many of them were the usual K class, but in 1871 twelve 0-6-0 tender engines were built for the 3ft 6in gauge. Exports continued until the end of the century, the last four being sent in 1899.

In Australia and New Zealand several main-line locomotives were exported, as well as many light industrial engines. Norway and Sweden used many small saddle tank engines which could commonly be seen in the works and docks at Christiana, later to become Oslo.

Manning Wardle developed a great variety of narrow gauge small locomotives for export including examples of 4-4-0T, 0-6-4T, 2-6-0T, 4-6-0T, 2-6-4T, and 2-8-2T that had not been built for the domestic market.

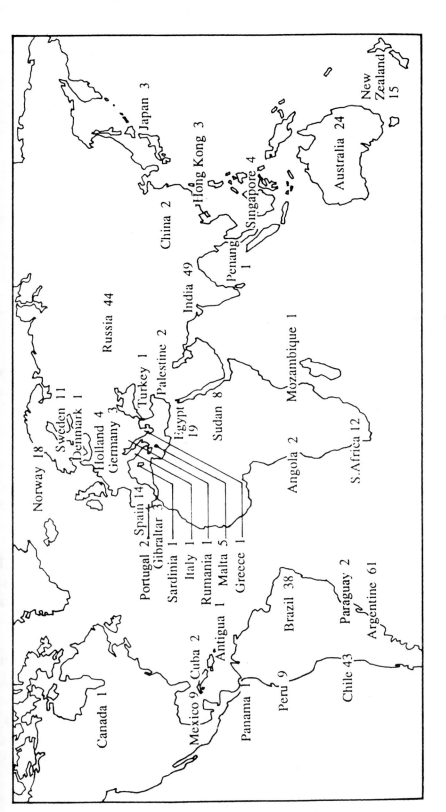

Figure 7.1 Manning Wardle locomotives sold abroad.

Argentina

In 1866 two F class 0-4-0ST, numbers 202 and 203 were sold to the Buenos Aires Western Railway. Fifty-nine other locomotives followed during the subsequent years until 1920. These were mostly small standard industrial saddle tank engines and some 0-6-0T. A few 4-4-0T were also exported (figure 7.2).

Figure 7.2 4-4-0T, No.8, MW no. 526 of 1875.
One of four supplied to E.Clark, Punchard & Company, contractors of Buenos Aires.
(photograph National Railway Museum)

Australia

From the earliest days of the Australian railways Manning Wardle exported locomotives there, eventually supplying a total of twenty-four. E.B.Wilson had sold 2-2-2 express engines of the Jenny Lynd type to the Commonwealth Railway in New South Wales and in 1860 three more of this type, numbers 8, 9, 10, were exported. Numbered 9, 10, 5N, they ran the main line service for five or six years until replaced by larger locomotives. Afterwards they continued in useful suburban and coal service for another twenty years.

A well-tank version of these locomotives had been produced by Wilson, but with smaller diameter driving wheels of 5ft 6ins instead of 5ft 9in. A similar engine to the three previously exported was works no. 11 of 1860. After a period hauling funeral trains at Sydney, No. 12, as she was numbered, was transferred to Bathurst. There she worked for many years until, after conversion to a crane engine, she was finally scrapped in 1900. A drawing is shown in figure 7.3.

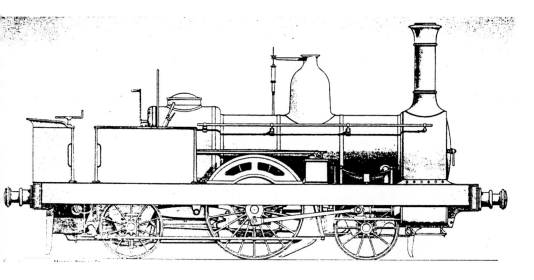

Figure 7.3 2-2-2WT, MW no.11 of 1860, No.12 of the New South Wales Railway.
(A.R.H.S., NSW branch)

Figure 7.4 4-4-0T, MW no. 39 of 1882. Built for the heavy coal traffic on the New South Wales Railway, she was transferred in 1891 to the East Greta Coal Mining Company and named *Daisy*.
(photograph A.R.H.S., NSW branch)

The two most powerful locomotives in New South Wales were ordered in 1882 from Manning Wardle to help with the expanding Newcastle coal traffic. These were 4-4-0T, works numbers 38, 39, numbered 6N, 7N by the Railway, and they provided a very useful service until 1890. No.6 (figure 7.4) was sold in 1891 to the East Greta Coal Mining Company and worked under the name of *Daisy* until scrapped in 1911.

Two other locomotives were constructed for New South Wales in 1862. These were 2-4-0 tender engines, works numbers 42 and 43, and they were used on secondary duties hauling passenger trains and mixed traffic. One of these handsome engines appears in figure 7.5, showing the similarity to the 'Crewe Goods' design, with double frames and crossheads between the frames.

Figure 7.5 2-4-0, MW no. 42 of 1862, built as No. 13 for the New South Wales Railway, later renumbered as No. 10. This engine worked trains on the Wallsend private railway, and after that was sold to Smith & Findlayson in 1890.
(photograph A.R.H.S., NSW branch)

Apart from these rather early unusual locomotives, many of the other exports to Australia consisted of small industrial 0-4-0ST and 0-6-0ST (figure 7.6). Most of these gave years of useful service, and some have been preserved, details of which are given in Chapter 8.

Figure 7.6 0-6-0ST, MW no. 739 of 1879, class N, No. 2 of the Caledonian Coal Company, Waratah Colliery, New South Wales.
(photograph J.A.Peden Collection).

Brazil

A total of thirty-eight locomotives were exported to Brazil. The earliest were the Pernambuco Tram engines which were later followed by the Fell mountain geared locomotives as described in Chapter 6.

Other locomotives sent to Brazil included numerous 0-4-0 and 0-6-0 types, but two unusual examples were *Imetiba*, 4-6-0T, works number 763 of 1880, for Rio de Janeiro and *Don Antonio*, 4-4-0T, works number 929, which went to Para in Brazil.

Chile

From as early as 1865 a total of forty-three locomotives were exported to Chile, many of which were K class 0-6-0ST.

One of the railways which was supplied was the 3ft 6in gauge Anglo-Chilean Nitrate and Railway Company, which climbed up from the coast into the Andes. This opened with four heavy Kitson 4-8-4T and one Manning Wardle 0-6-4T. The latter, works no. 1139 of 1889, was named *Edward Squire*.

Two Manning Wardle 0-4-0ST, works numbers 1107 and 1126 of 1889, were used during the construction of the line, and they stayed on and worked usefully for many years. One of these has been preserved and appears in Chapter 8.

Another narrow gauge railway with Manning Wardle locomotives was the 2ft 6in gauge Colorado Nitrate Company Railway (figure 7.7).

Figure 7.7 0-6-2T, MW no.1765 of 1910 of the Colorado Nitrate Company.
(photograph J.K.Williams Collection)

Egypt

Nineteen locomotives were built for Egypt. Figure 7.8 shows one of four 4-4-0T built for the narrow gauge Fayoud Railway in 1899. This was a 2ft 5in gauge network of lines operated by an Egyptian company built to carry agricultural traffic around the turn of the century. Four more locomotives were purchased in 1900, works numbers 1477-80. Some were still in service in 1945.

Figure 7.8. 4-4-0T, MW no. 1437 of 1889, built as No. 3 of the Fayoud Light Railway. (photograph R.N. & J.Redman Collection)

India

The first locomotives in India were built by E.B.Wilson for the Great Indian Penin-ular Railway of which fourteen 0-4-0T were used back-to-back on the Ghat incline n 1856. They also built the first main line passenger engines for the East India Railway in 1855 and 1886 which were 2-2-2, with 6ft 6in driving wheels.

For the broad gauge, Manning Wardle exported about twenty 0-4-0 and 0-6-0 saddle tank locomotives until as late as 1921. They also built locomotives for the Indian narrow gauge railways, especially on the 2ft 6in and the 2ft gauge lines. The Bengal-Nagpur Railway became the largest operator of such narrow gauge lines and four 0-6-2 engines were built in 1899 before it had been agreed that the 2ft 6in gauge should be the new standard. Upon arrival they were converted to the new gauge by the railway company (figure 7.9).

Figure 7.9 No.1H on the Fulwah-Islampur line, 26 Oct 1981.
(photograph Keith Chester)

Three very similar locomotives, but in tank engine form, were built twenty years later for the Fulwah-Islampur Light Railway. One of these was works no. 1921 of 1919 (figure 7.10).

Seven 0-4-2T were also exported for the 2ft gauge Howrah-Amta Railway and they operated on a service starting out from Calcutta.

Figure 7.10 0-6-2T, MW no. 1921 of 1919, built for the 2ft 6in gauge
Fulwah-Islampur Light Railway.
(photograph R.N.Redman Collection)

Figure 7.11 0-6-2T, MW no. 1919 of 1919 struggles to make steam on a Hugh Ballantyne
Railway Enthusiasts Special over the 2ft 6in gauge Fulwah-Islampur Light Railway.
(photograph H.Holdsworth)

Japan

In 1871 Japan's first railway, the 3ft 6in gauge Imperial Railway, opened from Shinbashi to Yokahama with a locomotive built by the Vulcan Foundry. Later three 0-6-0ST engines were imported from Manning Wardle, the first two arriving in 1873. They were used for railway construction in many places, including the Kyoto-Kobe line before both were transferred to Chiba prefecture and used for public transport until 1930. One of these is illustrated in figure 7.12.

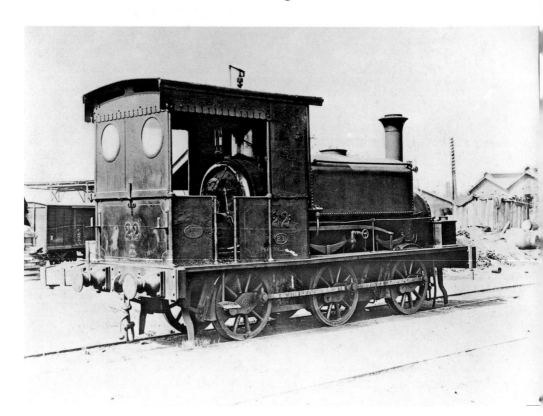

Figure 7.12 One of the first two 0-6-0ST locomotives exported to Japan in 1873, MW no. 431 of 1873.

The third locomotive to arrive, works no. 815 of 1881, was used in the construction of the Tokyo-Aomori line, built by the first private Japanese railway company, the Nippon Railway Company. This locomotive was named *Zenko* after the name of a temple in the town where it first landed in Japan. It remained in service until 1923 and was later transferred to the Transport Museum in Tokyo.

Figure 7.13 0-6-0ST, *Zenko*, MW no. 815 of 1881, one of the three Manning Wardle locomotives which worked in Japan. This is commemorated by a postage stamp (see Chapter 8).

Malta

The Malta Railway was metre gauge, seven-and-a-half miles long. It was opened in 1882 with three special Manning Wardle 0-6-0T, works numbers 842, 843, 844. They were numbered 1, 2, and 3, and the first of these is shown in figure 7.14.

Soon after the service began it was obvious that another more powerful engine was needed and a larger 0-6-0ST, No. 4, was purchased from Black Hawthorn of Gateshead. This had a long saddle tank and a spark-arrestor chimney, but was later completely rebuilt.

After only five years it became apparent that continual mismanagement had ruined the engines. Two of the three Manning Wardle engines were unfit for service and later the boiler of No. 4 exploded while the train was in the Floriana Tunnel. The service was then suspended and the Government took over the Railway. Nos. 1, 2,

3 were reboilered, and two much larger locomotives, No. 5 and 6, were ordered. The invoice for No. 6, made out to the Crown Agents from the Boyne Engine Works is shown in figure 7.15.

The first of these two, works no. 1243, was built as a 2-6-2T in 1891 but suffered from numerous technical problems. It was hoped rebuilding as a 2-6-4T would provide a solution and both No. 5 and No. 6 were modified in this way, but the results were disappointing. Four more 2-6-4T from Beyer Peacock followed and proved to be more successful.

Figure 7.14 Malta Railway No. 1, 0-6-0, MW no. 842 of 1882.
(photograph J.K.Williams Collection)

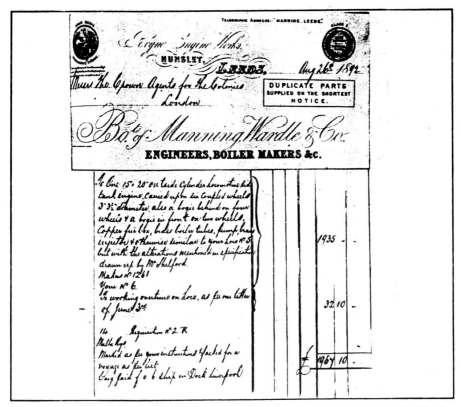

Figure 7.15 Copy of the invoice from Manning Wardle at the Boyne Engine Works
to the Crown Agents for the 2-6-4T, No. 6, for the Malta Railway.

When the railway was closed in 1931, one of the earlier locomotives, No. 2, was still
being employed on secondary off-peak trains. It later took pride of place on a commemorative postage stamp (figure 7.16).

Figure 7.16 A commemorative stamp, celebrating the centenary of the opening of the
Malta Railway, featuring a Manning Wardle 0-6-0ST.

New Zealand

In 1865 the 4ft 8½in gauge Auckland & Drury Railway ordered 0-6-0ST, *Driver*, works no. 162, an old I class locomotive. However, when work on the railway ceased she was put into storage for five years and then sold to the Bay of Islands Coal Company for work on a short railway at Kawakawa.

Figure 7.17 An artist's impression of MW no. 162 of 1865, No.1, *Driver*, built for the Auckland and Drury Railway.
(by W.W.Stewart)

Manning Wardle also built the original main line locomotives for the 3ft 6in gauge Wellington & Manawata Railway. These were five 2-6-2T, works numbers 920-4, built in 1884. They were very successful engines after some early teething troubles had been overcome by extending the front of the smoke-box. For many years they worked the Wellington and Paekariki line, and sometimes as many as three of these engines were used to lift a single train over the steep gradient. Figure 7.18 shows one before the smoke-box extension.

Figure 7.18 MW no. 922 of 1884, 2-6-2T, of the 3ft 6in gauge Wellington & Manawatu Railway.
This was taken before the smoke-box had been extended.
(photograph R.C.Riley Collection)

Figure 7.19 MW no. 1753 of 1909, *Dominion*, a 2ft 9in gauge 4-4-2T
of the Waiki Gold Mining Company, New Zealand.
(photograph R.N.Redman Collection)

Locomotives were exported to the 2ft 6in narrow gauge Waiki Gold Mining Company's railway in North Island, New Zealand. These included, in 1897 and 1898, a small 0-4-0ST and an 0-4-2ST. They were followed in 1905 and 1909 by two much larger engines, one of which is shown in figure 7.19.

Some standard industrial locomotives were also exported to New Zealand. Two of the 0-4-0ST have been preserved in working order, one at Palmerston North in North Island and one at Christchurch in South Island. These are described in Chapter 8 which deals with preserved engines.

Norway

Figure 7.20 MW 0-4-0ST, no. 1248 of 1892, in Oslo, No.11, of the Norwegian State Railways.

Eighteen small F class, 0-4-0ST industrial locomotives were exported to Norway These were mostly employed in shunting around the docks in Christiania, now Oslo Two of them still exist. The first, MW no. 576 of 1877 stands in the Centra

Station in Oslo still showing the large cab built for use in cold weather. The other one, MW no. 1428 of 1892, has been rebuilt in working order and can be seen in action on an enthusiasts railway.

Paraguay

Figure 7.21 shows the works photograph of a narrow gauge 2-8-2WT built in 1916. This was supplied via Percy Grant & Company of Buenos Aires for service in Paraguay. This was for the 2ft 6in gauge railway that ran from Puerto Casado, carrying logs to the capital Asunción which is close to the Argentine border.

Figure 7.21 2-8-2WT, MW no. 1901 of 1916, No. 5, *Don Carlos*,
of Compañia Carlos Casado, Paraguay.(photograph R.N.Redman Collection)

The 2-8-2WT, No. 5 *Don Carlos* was photographed by Colin Garratt on an expedition to Paraguay in 1978 when this locomotive was still working at Puerto Casado in company with a Baldwin 2-8-2WT.

Peru

Eight locomotives were sent to Peru. The most extraordinary of these was no. 246 of 1868, a small 3ft 6in gauge saddle tank locomotive with the unusual 4-2-0 wheel arrangement (figure 7.22). It seems that this engine was designed to run on a railway from Callao to sugar estates in Lima, with curves so sharp that the provision of a front bogie was necessary. Black Hawthorn & Company supplied other locomotives of the same wheel arrangement, but these were more powerful and had larger cylinders.

Figure 7.22 4-2-0ST, MW no. 246 of 1868. This was designed for a 3ft 6in gauge railway in Peru (photograph Locomotive Magazine)

Portugal

Manning Wardle built a most impressive 3ft 6in gauge 2-2-6-0T for Mason & Barry Ltd, of São Domingos in Portugal, works no. 1830 of 1913. Used to haul traffic between the quarries and copper mines of São Domingos and the port of Pomarão ten miles away, this powerful engine dealt well with an undulating line that included a short length of 1 in 18. A repeat order was placed the following year and works no. 1856, *Algarve*, was built.

Figure 7.23 2-6-0T, MW no. 1856 of 1914, *Algarve*, hauling a train of 26 'tubs' up the steep gradient out of Salgueiros.
(photograph J.K.Williams)

Russia

A total of forty-four locomotives were exported to Russia; twenty-one were of 5ft gauge, twelve on 3ft 6in gauge, ten on 3ft gauge, and a single example of 1ft 6in gauge.

The first to arrive was an old I class 0-6-0ST, works no. 105 of 1864, on the 5ft gauge, sent to Peto & Betts & Company, contractors of Riga. Five more similar

0-6-0 saddle tanks followed in the same year and two years later, two K class engines arrived.

In 1871 a batch of twelve 0-6-0 tender engines were purchased by the 3ft 6 in gauge Yaroslav & Volagda Railway that was being developed in the region north of Moscow. These had works numbers from 354 to 365. One of them is shown in figure 7.24.

Figure 7.24 0-6-0, MW no. 364 of 1871 on the Yaroslav-Vologda Railway.
(photograph Finnish Railways Museum)

In 1875 a 1ft 6in gauge 0-4-0ST, works no. 734, (CHT), was sent to Easton & Anderson of St. Petersberg. Another single order of 1890 was for a class E, 0-4-0ST, no. 734 of 1890, from General Falbelhagen at Poti.

The remainder of the Russian exports were during the 1890s and were all 0-4-0ST or 0-6-0ST on either 5ft or 3ft 6in gauge for the New Russia Company based in the centre of the iron industry in the Donetz Basin. The last four were sent in 1899 works numbers 1451-1454.

Figure 7.25 A Manning Wardle locomotive at a Russian ironworks in 1914.
Note the number of women engaged in manual work. (photograph A.Kolesov Collection)

Spain

Three different railways in Spain had Manning Wardle locomotives at various times on both narrow and standard gauges.

Firstly, six engines were sent in the 1890s to the 3ft 6in gauge line near Malaga in southern Spain. The Cartagena and Herrerías Steam Tramway Co. Ltd was originally a British company and their export orders included the ubiquitous K class 0-6-0ST and some outside cylinder 0-6-0T. In 1897 the railway reached Los Blancos and became the F.C. de Cartagena a La Unión y Los Blancos. Figure 7.26 shows K class 0-6-0ST, *Nueva Lucia*.

The second narrow-gauge railway was the F.C. Económico de Cortés a Borja, west of Zaragoza, which received two 0-6-0 side tank locomotives, works numbers 1095 and 1096 of 1888. One of these engines, *Aragon*, is shown in figure 7.27. The line was closed in 1955.

Figure 7.26 0-6-0ST, MW no. 1007 of 1887, *Nueva Lucia*,
built for the 3ft 6in gauge Cartagena & Herrerías Steam Tramway.
(photograph the Hunslet Engine Co. Ltd)

Figure 7.27 0-6-0T, MW no. 1095 of 1888, *Aragon* No.1,
on the F.C. Económico de Cortés a Borja.
(photograph the Hunslet Engine Co. Ltd)

The third railway on the north coast was the standard gauge Bilbao & Cantabrian Railway, and four Manning Wardle 0-4-0ST were built between 1873 and 1887, together with seven Kitson 4-6-0T. No other locomotives were taken in stock and some of the Manning Wardle saddle tanks carried on until the line was closed in 1970.

Figure 7.28 0-6-0ST, MW no. 658 of 1877, at Bilbao in 1965.
(photograph J.K.Williams)

CHAPTER EIGHT

Preserved Locomotives

As many as thirty-six of the two thousand Manning Wardle locomotives built have been preserved in some form or other, a fair proportion of the total. In the few countries that still have active groups of railway enthusiasts - mostly in Britain, but also some in New Zealand and Norway - a proportion have been preserved as working locomotives. In Britain, not only comparatively recent engines built in the 1920s, but some very early locomotives have been carefully restored into working order.

Several preserved 0-6-0ST locomotives are undergoing restoration by small working groups, and a project has been established to build a complete replica narrow-gauge 2-6-2T of the type originally built for the Lynton & Barnstaple Railway.

What follows is a series of photographs and notes on most of the preserved Manning Wardle locomotives in approximate chronological order.

Norway

In 1875 when the Norwegian Trunk Railway required some shunting engines, they ordered their first two Manning Wardle locomotives, works numbers 550 and 576. Ten others followed, all giving many years useful service and known as the ULKA class - not an especially attractive name, being a kind of squat catfish.

Eventually only two of these little engines still existed and it was decided they should be preserved. The oldest, No.25, was put on a plinth at the Oslo Central Station, while the younger, No.11, was taken over by a group of enthusiasts to be put into working order on the Króderbanen Railway.

Figure 8.1 The oldest preserved Manning Wardle locomotive at the Central Station in Oslo. This is No.25, MW no.576 of 1875, class F, 0-4-0ST, the first of the twelve purchased by Norway.
(photograph by the author)

The last time that No.11, works no.1248 of 1892 had been under steam was in 1970 when she was used in the making of a film. The restoration had started in December 1984, masterminded by David Bartos, an Englishman who had lived in Norway for many years and helped by his son, Paul Christian and other volunteers. In January 1987 the work was transferred to the State Railway workshop at Drammen and the rebuilding was complete by July 1989 when the locomotive left the paintshop. She was then in the condition shown in figure 8.2.

Two obvious changes were made to the cab and to the chimney. They were re-constructed according to the original drawings and also partly from early photographs supplied by the author. The original maker's number plates went missing about 1964 and could not be traced, and copies had to be made from No.25 using dental surgery techniques.

The first successful run was made on the Króder railway on 29 July 1989, and a view of her in full steam hauling a train of two carriages is shown in figure 8.3.

Figure 8.2 No 11, MW no.1248 of 1892 after rebuilding was complete.

Figure 8.3 Restored 0-4-0ST, MW no.1248 of 1892 hauling a train
on the Króder railway, 29 July 1989. David Bartos can be seen on the footplate.
(photograph Torgeir Aas)

The Oldest Preserved 0-6-0ST

The oldest Manning Wardle locomotive preserved in Britain is a K class 0-6-0ST no.641 of 1877. Under the name of *Solomon*, it was originally owned by Charles Deacon of Kettering. After spending her early days working as a contractor's locomotive for three other firms, she was bought by Samuel Williams & Son of Dagenham Docks, where she became No.4 (figure 8.4). Williams & Son had a fleet of small shunting engines, of which no less than six were built by Manning Wardle and many of them were still working in the 1950s. As these were withdrawn one at a time, the company decided to preserve the gem of the collection, No.4. At first she spent some years *'silent on a plinth in Dagenham'*, as shown in figure 8.5.

Figure 8.4 MW no.641 of 1877, working as No.4 at Samuel Williams & Son Ltd., Dagenham.
(photograph Eric Sawford)

In 1970 this engine moved to Blooms of Bressingham where I saw her painted green, still with the large polished works plate of the Dagenham Docks. In 1984 she was bought by the Bluebell Railway for static display and now carries the appropriate nameplate *Sharpthorn*, previously borne when working for Joseph Firbank on the construction of the Lewis and East Grinstead Railways.

Figure 8.5 No.4 of the Dagenham Docks, MW no.641 of 1877, preserved on a plinth at Dagenham, 1965. She is wearing the light blue livery acquired in 1958.
(photograph Peter Heath)

Figure 8.6 0-6-0ST, *Sharpthorn*, MW no.641 of 1877 at the Bluebell Railway in 1986.
(photograph J.K.Williams)

Japan

Figure 8.7 0-6-0ST, MW no.816 of 1882, preserved at Tokyo.

Figure 8.8 MW no.816 of 1882, preserved in the Transportation Museum at Tokyo, bearing her Japanese National Railways number, 1292. (photography R.Kimura)

A very early Manning Wardle 0-6-0ST is preserved at the Transportation Museum in Tokyo. This is No.1, *Zenko*, works no.816 of 1882, built on the 3ft 6in gauge for the Imperial Railway of Japan (figure 8.7 and 8.8). This locomotive has been commemorated by a postage stamp (figure 8.9).

Figure 8.9 Postage stamp of 1982, commemorating Manning Wardle 0-6-0ST, issued in Japan.

Another home-based K Class 0-6-0ST

Manning Wardle works no.865 of 1883, a K Class 0-6-0ST, at one time worked at Lucas & Air contractors in Maidstone. After two other contractors jobs, she then began to work for the Air Ministry: first at Kenley and then later at Kidbrooke in south-east London. Here she bore the name *Aldwyth* and the number 339 (figure 8.10).

After many years working for the Ministry of Aviation, she was withdrawn and taken over by Mr Robin Dean to work on his projected Usk Valley Railway. This was to run about three-quarters of a mile from his Manor House to the River Usk. She lay in the undergrowth near the Manor House for some years (figure 8.11).

Figure 8.10 0-6-0ST, MW no.865 of 1883, K Class working at the Air Ministry, Kidbrooke. (photograph J.P.Mullett)

Figure 8.11 MW no.865 of 1883, *Aldwyth* lying in the bushes, awaiting the regeneration of the Usk River Railway.

After the death of Mr Dean, *Aldwyth* passed to the Armley Mill Industrial Museum at Leeds, where she has been beautifully restored for static display. She still bears the plate on the smoke-box *RAF No.111*.

Figure 8.12 MW no.865 of 1883, *Aldwyth* on display at the Armley Mills Industrial Museum. (photograph by the author)

Zaire

Manning Wardle built a 'special' 0-6-0ST with outside cylinders on the 3ft 6in gauge, which spent most of its time in Zaire. This was no.1656 of 1905 and was delivered to contractors Pauling and Company at Beira.

It was used by Paulings on the construction of the railway north of Livingstone and was named *Maramba* after a small river which runs into the Zambesi. From there it moved up the then Belgian Congo and is said to have been the first locomotive in Katanga. Later it was stored in the workshops at Lubumbashi eventually to be on permanent display outside the administrative offices (figure 8.13).

A South American centenarian

The Anglo-Chilean Nitrate Railway Company was mentioned in Chapter 7 as having Manning Wardle 0-6-4T and 0-4-0ST locomotives. The two 0-4-0ST worked on the construction of the railway in 1889 and then continued to be used on it for many years. After working as shed shunter, one of these engines, works no.1126 of 1889 was preserved on retirement and is shown in figure 8.14.

Figure 8.13 0-6-0ST, MW no.1656 of 1905, 3ft 6in gauge, preserved at Lubumbashi, Zaire.
(photograph P.F.Bagstawe)

Figure 8.14 MW no.1126 of 1889, preserved at Tocopilla, in 1993.
(photograph J.K.Williams)

Zimbabwe: the Victoria Falls locomotive

Originally this Manning Wardle 0-6-0ST, works no.1159 of 1889, was of 3ft gauge and owned by the English contractor J.P.Williams who was building the Dore to Chinley branch line, part of the Midland Railway. The engine was altered to 3ft 6in gauge and shipped to Paulings at Beita. In 1900 the Mashonaland Railway bought the engine which then became their No.7.

For many years the engine named *Jack Tar* shunted at the docks at Beira, being the only one light enough to cross the bridge to the Customs wharf.

Figure 8.15 MW no.1159 of 1889, *Jack Tar*, of the Mashonaland Railway
that worked at the docks at Beira.

During 1904-5 *Jack Tar* was sent to Victoria Falls for use during the construction of the famous bridge. One night while hauling trucks to the north bank, its side-rod killed a leopard that had strayed onto the uncompleted bridge and was crouching beside the track. During its career the engine distinguished itself by being the first locomotive to cross the new bridge.

When the bridge was finished, *Jack Tar* returned to shunting duties at Beira. In 1937 a new boiler was fitted with a new brass dome and chimney cap, and a new fully enclosed cab. In 1942 the little locomotive was moved to Umtali for light shunting duties until withdrawn for preservation. Exhibited at the Rhodes Centenary Exhibition in 1953, it is now in the Railway Museum at Bulawayo.

Success Story - *Sir Berkeley*

Figure 8.16 MW no.1210 of 1890 when she was No.30 of Logan & Hemingway, later to be preserved under the name *Sir Berkeley*. (photograph Nottinghamshire County Concil)

Manning Wardle no.1210 of 1890 is an L class 0-6-0ST. For many years this locomotive worked for Logan and Hemingway of Chesterfield on different railway construction projects, initially as No.30 on the M.S. & L.R in Nottinghamshire, later as No.10 on the Great Central extension to London, and then on the GWR Westbury & Frome avoiding line between 1931 and 1933. Figure 8.16 is an early photograph of her in the Nottingham Joint Station excavation site.

The locomotive was rebuilt by Manning Wardle in 1910, and in 1935 was sold to the Cranford Ironstone Company in Northampton. Soon after joining the Ironstone works, the engine, which had always been known unofficially as *Paddy Logan*, acquired the name *Sir Berkeley* from another Manning Wardle that had been scrapped.

Figure 8.17 0-6-0ST Manning Wardle class L, *Sir Berkeley*,
active at the Middleton Railway in 1996.
(photograph by the author)

In the early 1950s Manning Wardle number 1210 underwent a complete renewal during which the original weather-board was replaced by an open-backed cab. She was still working at Cranford in the early 1960s. When due to be scrapped in 1963 the engine was purchased by Mr R.Crombleholme and moved to Haworth on the K & WVR. Here she was run occasionally until a complete rebuild was undertaken by the Vintage Carriage Trust. This included refitting the original weather-board that was found at Cranford.

In her new active state she has visited several other railways, and my photograph, (figure 8.17), shows her on the Middleton Railway in 1996.

Arthur

This 0-6-0ST of class L started life as a contractor's engine with J.Aird & Company, working initially next to the Austin Motor Works at Longbridge, and then at the A.P.C.M. Kent works at Stone near Greenhithe.

Figure 8.18 MW no.1601 of 1903, class L, at Kent works, Stone.
(photograph R.C.Riley Collection)

Arthur is preserved at the Middleton Railway where I took this photograph (figure 8.19) of the engine undergoing a heavy overhaul in 1986. When this overhaul was finished in 1987 it was hoped, with *Sir Berkeley*, to have two Manning Wardle saddle-tank engines at work together on the Middleton Railway. However this was not to be because, after trial steaming, it was decided that *Arthur* needed a new boiler barrel.

When finally complete, *Arthur* is to be renamed *Matthew Murray* No.3, following a tradition for Manning Wardle locomotives at Middleton.

Figure 8.19. MW no.1601 of 1903, *Arthur*, undergoing an overhaul
at the Middleton Railway workshops.
(photograph by the author)

Australia

The three Australian examples are all in the Sydney district. The oldest is works number 1781 of 1911, one of two purchased by the New South Wales Department of Public Works. After working on various railways and tramways, the two were bought by the Metropolitan Water Sewerage and Drainage Board, and after 1923 were used at the Ryde Water Pumping Station. After forty productive years there, number 1781 was earmarked for preservation and moved to museum storage in 1966, and later was restored to operating condition. The photograph in figure 8.20 shows her at the museum's Castle Hill Store, awaiting return to steam in a future Powerhouse exhibition.

Figure 8.20 MW no.1781 of 1911 in store at Castle Hill Museum, Haymarket, Sydney, in 1990, awaiting its return to steam.

The next preserved Australian locomotive is 0-4-0ST, works no.1802, with the name *Possum*. She was originally named *Cyclops* and worked in England for five years at Barrow-in-Furness. When purchased by G.C.Hoskins Ltd, *Possum* worked at Lithgow Iron Works until she was transferred to the Australian Iron & Steel at Port Kembla in 1928. Withdrawn from service at Port Kembla in 1967, *Possum* was presented to the Lithgow District Historical Museum in 1969 (figure 8.21).

Manning Wardle 0-4-0ST, works no.1896 *Cardiff,* was one of five of this type imported by the New South Wales Public Works Department in 1916. This engine was then called *The Baby Singer*, named after a small make of very popular Singer sewing machines. While the other four were ceded to the Railway Department, this one stayed and became No.1212. After spending some time on the Marrangaroo deviation, the engine was then renumbered 1021. About 1929 it is said that a certain locomotive superintendent saw this little engine standing forlorn and forgotten in a siding while on a fishing holiday. He had the engine sent to Cardiff where it was overhauled and became a works shunter. In 1949 it was used at the Enfield round-house for steam cleaning purposes. In 1952 it appeared in royal blue livery as the works shunter at Cardiff, with the name *Cardiff* on the saddle tanks. During the 1970s it was again at Cardiff in a relieving capacity before finally reaching the New South Wales Transport Museum at Thirlemere, New South Wales.

Figure 8.21 0-4-0ST, *Possum*, MW no 1802 of 1912,
at the Lithgow District Historical Society Museum.

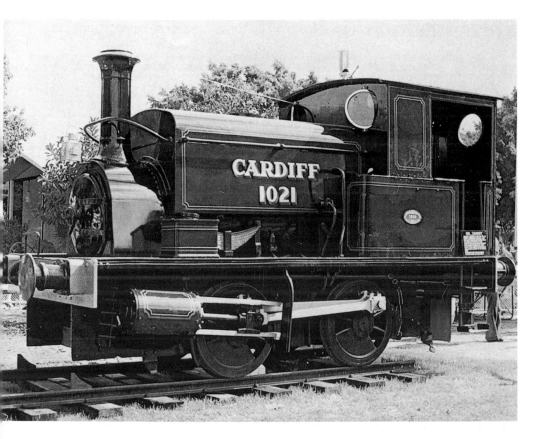

Figure 8.22 0-4-0ST MW no 1896 of 1916 *Cardiff*, one of five bought
by the New South Wales Public Works Department. After a long and varied career
this engine is preserved at the New South Wales Transport Museum at Thirlemere.

New Zealand

Manning Wardle 0-4-0ST no.1841 of 1914 was bought by the Christchurch Meat
Company and later worked at the Waitaki Refrigerating Company at their Islington
Works. She is now preserved and active at the Ferrymead Historic Park, Christchurch
(figure 8.23).

Another 3ft 6in gauge 0-4-0ST is preserved in New Zealand seventy miles north of
Wellington on the North Island. *WEKA* no.1890 of 1916, class E, was also sold to the
Christchurch Meat Company. Later she worked at the New Zealand Refrigerating
Company at Imlay, and is now preserved at the Tokamaru Steam engine museum

at Palmerston North. Figure 8.24 shows her on a centenary celebration run.

Figure 8.23 0-4-0ST, MW no 1841 of 1914, class E,
working at the Ferrymead Railway, Christchurch, New Zealand.
(photograph C.Dash)

Figure 8.24 0-4-0ST, *WEKA*, MW no.1890 of 1916, class E, preserved on the
Tokamaru Steam Railway at Palmerston North, New Zealand.

Two narrow gauge locomotives

The Penrhyn Quarry in North Wales operated on many different levels where the slate was hauled by numerous small 1ft 11in gauge locomotives. As part of the Jubilee celebrations of Queen Victoria, a new 0-4-0ST Manning Wardle locomotive was bought, works no.1382, and named *Jubilee 1897*. This has been preserved as a static display in the Narrow Gauge Railway Museum at Tywyn Station on the Talyllyn Railway.

Figure 8.25 1ft 11in gauge 0-4-0ST, MW no 1382, *Jubilee 1897*, now preserved at Tywyn Station. Seen here in 1935 at work in the Penrhyn Quarry.
(photograph by the author)

The Kettering Iron and Coal Company ran an extensive 3ft gauge railway that has previously been described. When the railway closed in 1949 the company's three Manning Wardle locomotives were still operating, and the most recent, No 8, works no 1675 of 1906, has been preserved. It was initially in the Kettering Museum, but has recently had to undergo an extensive overhaul at the Welland Valley Traction Club, Market Harborough (figure 8.26).

Figure 8.26 3ft gauge 0-6-0ST, MW no 1675 of 1906,
seen here as No.8 of the Kettering Iron and Coal Company.
(photograph R.T.Russell of the National Railway Museum)

Private Preservation

Manning Wardle works no.1532 of 1901 was an M class 0-6-0ST that started life at the Midland Coal Coke & Iron Co. Ltd at their Apedale Ironworks. During the war she worked with the Ministry of Munitions and then with Wilson Lovatt & Son Ltd at Wolverhampton.In 1927 she was loaned to the British Sugar Corporation at Ely and later worked at the Kings Lynn Factory. After some time on the Wissington Light Railway in 1972 she was moved for preservation to a private location near Royston, Herts.

Figure 8.27 0-6-0ST MW no 1532 of 1901 at the Wissington Light Railway.
(photograph Eric Sawford)

Static display locomotives in Britain

Very few Manning Wardle locomotives are still preserved in the open but some have been cosmetically preserved in museums.

An example that can be found standing in the open is 0-6-0ST, *Winston Churchill*, works no.2025 of 1923. Formally working as a colliery engine in Darlington, it moved to Shut End Colliery and was later bought by Cadbury's for its Bournville Works. After becoming redundant, it was purchased by the Pensnett Industrial Estate in the West Midlands and now stands by one of the minor roads on the estate.

Another Manning Wardle 0-6-0ST, works no.2010 of 1921, also stands in a rather improbable site. This engine was No.42 *Rhondda* which spent most of its life in different iron works and quarries in the Corby district, now stands outside Castor Castle forming part of a Transport Museum.

A preserved 0-4-0ST

Only one example of the once universal small 0-4-0ST has been preserved in its country of origin, although several of them are preserved abroad. This is No.14, works no.1795 of 1916, class P which was purchased by T.W.Ward of Sheffield. After working for four other owners, she went to the Northampton Ironstone Railway Trust at Hunsbury Hill and was named *Brill*.

The photograph in figure 8.28 shows her in steam in 1977, but since then she has fallen on hard times and a return to action seems unlikely.

Figure 8.28 0-4-0ST, *Brill*, MW no.1795 of 1912, P class,
at the Northampton Ironstone Railway at Hunsbury Hill, Northampton.

Currently being restored

Until 1930, *The Welshman,* a long-boiler type 0-6-0ST Manning Wardle, works no.1207 of 1890, was used at the Llay Hall Colliery. Various other work followed before finally being preserved at the Chatterley Whitfield Mining Museum, Turnstall, Stoke on Trent. Unfortunately this museum went into liquidation and *The Welshman* is now at the Caphouse Mining Museum in Yorkshire.

Manning Wardle had rebuilt the engine in 1922 with a fully enclosed cab, and later a coal bunker was fitted and the side tank removed. Figure 8.29 shows the engine in its original condition. Currently it is being restored to working order.

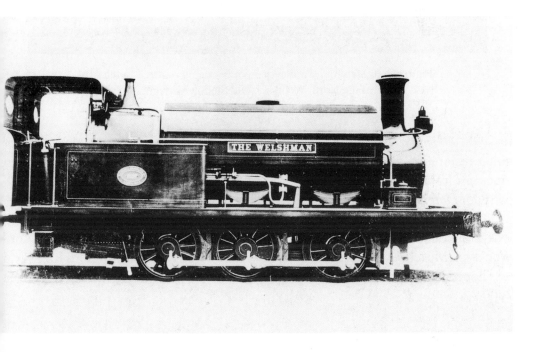

Figure 8.29 *The Welshman*, MW no.1207 of 1890 in its original condition.

Presently eight other preserved Manning Wardle locomotives, some removed from their plinths, are being restored to working order by small groups of devoted workers.

Figure 8.30 Manning Wardle locomotives being restored in the yard
of the North Woolwich Old Station Museum.
(photograph by the author)

In 1998, *Abernant* was at the North Woolwich Old Station Museum, slowly undergoing restoration alongside three other Manning Wardle 0-6-0ST. These other engines, all from Stewart & Lloyds Corby Ironstone Works, were *Rhiwnant*, no.131?
of 1895, *Dolobran*, no.1762 of 1910, and *Rhyl*, no.2009 of 1921.

It was announced in January 1999 that the locomotives in the yard of the North
Woolwich Museum would be transferred to the Cholsey and Wallingford Railway. I
was hoped that at least one of these engines would be in steam by the end of the yea
2000.

Locomotives operating on steam railways in England

The last four Manning Wardle locomotives to be illustrated have been operating
regularly on well-established steam railways in England. These are the Whipsnade
and Umfolozi Railway, the Kent & East Sussex Light Railway, the Avon Valley
Railway, and the Severn Valley Railway.

Whipsnade and Umfolozi Railway

The narrow-gauge 0-6-2T design was exported all over the world, and fortunately one example has been preserved here, working on the Whipsnade and Umfolozi Railway in Whipsnade Zoo.

Manning Wardle works no.1877 of 1915, O-6-2T No.1 *Chevallier* was built for the Admiralty to work on the 2ft 6in gauge Chattendon & Upnor Railway in Essex. In 1950 she moved to the Bowater Lloyd Pulp and Paper Mills at Sittingbourne, Kent (figure 8.31). Bowaters operated an extensive 2ft 6in gauge railway throughout their works and had other 0-6-2T engines. Some were built by Bagnalls and these often had spark-arrestor chimneys, but one was never fitted to *Chevallier*.

Figure 8.31 0-6-2T, MW no.1877 of 1915, *Chevallier*,
working as No.1 at Bowaters at Sittingbourne.
(photograph Eric Sawford)

In 1968 while awaiting an overhaul, the engine was bought by Sir William McAlpine, a Fellow of the Zoological Society and a railway enthusiast. In 1970 *Chevallier* hauled the first train on the newly formed Whipsnade and Umfolozi Railway, carrying passengers around Whipsnade Park.

Figure 8.32 *Chevallier* still at work on what is now named the Great Whipsnade Railway. The railway of 2ft gauge has two other 0-6-2T from Bowaters at Sittingbourne. (photograph Ian Gordon)

Kent & East Sussex Light Railway

The Kent & East Sussex Light Railway was one of the most interesting managed by Colonel Stephens, and it owned one Manning Wardle saddle-tank engine that was partly disguised by its Swindon rebuild. The KESR was reopened as a preservation society in 1974, and is fortunate enough to have an operational 0-6-0ST Manning Wardle locomotive, number 1955 of 1918, *Charwelton*. This worked at the Charwelton Ironstone, Northants, and later at Sproxton Quarries, Lincolnshire. It has now become a working member of the team of various engines on this railway.

Figure 8.33. 0-6-0ST MW no.1955 of 1918 hauling a train on the Kent & East Sussex Railway. (photograph K.E.S.R. Collection, Euslin Bruce)

Avon Valley Railway

The Avon Valley Railway, based at Bitton Station between Bristol and Bath, is a working museum devoted to the operation of steam locomotives. Several main line steam engines are maintained and there is also a collection of industrial locomotives, including a Manning Wardle. This 0-6-0ST, works no.2018 of 1922, was *Litteton No 5*, and originally it operated at the Littleton Colliery Company in Cannock. In 1947 it went to work for the National Coal Board in the West Midlands and was later put aside for preservation.

Figure 8.34 0-6-0ST *Littleton No.5* in operation on the Avon Valley Railway in 1995.
(photograph Avon Valley Railway)

Severn Valley Railway

The Severn Valley Railway, with stations at Bridgnorth and Kidderminster hosts more main line engines than any other preserved line in the country. Industrial locomotives on this line include *Warwickshire*, number 2047 of 1926, the last Manning Wardle locomotive built.

This engine worked at the Rugby Portland Cement Company, New Bilton Works, until purchased in 1968 by the Warwickshire Industrial Locomotive Trust. Now kept at Bridgnorth, she is illustrated in figure 8.35.

Figure 8.35 MW no.2047 of 1926, *Warwickshire* at Bridgnorth on the Severn Valley Railway. (photograph N.Cripps, W.I.L.T. Collection)

For the last photograph of a preserved Manning Wardle locomotive in this book, I am happy to be able to include a fine shot of *Warwickshire* blasting out of Bridgnorth on a works train of the Severn Railway.

Figure 8.36 MW no. 2047 of 1926, *Warwickshire* recreating the past on the
Severn Valley Railway.
(photograph D.C.Williams, W.I.L.T. Collection)

Table of Preserved Locomotives

Works number	Year	Type	Name	Location
576	1877	0-4-0ST		NSB Central Station Oslo, Norway
641	1877	0-6-0ST	Sharpthorn	Bluebell Railway
815	1882	0-6-0ST	Zenko	Tokyo Transport Museum
865	1883	0-6-0ST	Aldwyth	Armley Mills Industrial Museum, Leeds
1045	1887	0-6-0ST	42	Park near Central Station Montevideo, Uruguay
1126	1889	0-4-0-ST	7	Tocopilla, Chile
1159	1890	0-6-0-ST	Jack Tar	Zimbabwe Railway Museum Bulawayo
1198	1890	0-6-0ST	No.3	Docks Port Authority Montevideo, Uruguay
1207	1890	0-6-0ST	The Welshman	Caphouse Mining Museum
1210	1890	0-6-0ST	Sir Berkeley	Vintage Carriage Trust Hawarth, W.Yorks
1248	1892	0-4-0ST	11	Rebuilt by David Bartos Kroderbahn Norway
1317	1895	0-6-0ST	35 Rhiwnant	Cholsey & Wallingford Railway
1382	1897	0-4-0ST	Jubilee 1897	Narrow Gauge Railway Museum, Tywyn
1472	1900	0-4-0ST	Gervase	Rosco (Railways) Ltd Woolwich (Reb. Sentinel)
1532	1901	0-6-0ST	Newcastle	Cambs.Lt. Ry, Royston
1583	1902	0-4-0ST	Midge	Johannesburg Mining Museum, S.Africa
1601	1901	0-6-0ST	Arthur	Middleton Railway, Leeds
1656	1905	0-6-0ST	1 Maramba	Lubumbashi, SNCF Zaire

1675	1906	0-6-0ST	8	Welland Valley Vintage Traction Club Market Harborough
1762	1910	0-6-0ST	38 Dolobran	Cholsey & Wallingford Railway
1781	1911	0-4-0ST	4	Powerhouse, Haymarket, Sydney, Australia
1795	1916	0-4-0ST	Brill	Northampton Ironstone Railway Trust Co Hunsbury Hill
1802	1912	0-4-0ST	Possum	Lithgow Historical Society Eskbank Museum Lithgow, Australia
1841	1914	0-4-0ST		Ferrybank Trust, Christchurch, N.Zealand
1864	1915	0-4-0ST	10	Museum of Sierra Leone Cline Town
1877	1915	0-6-2T	Chevallier	Whipsnade & Umfolozi Ry Whipsnade Zoo
1890	1916	0-4-0ST	Weka	Tokamaru Steam Engine Mus. Palmerston N, N.Z.
1896	1916	0-4-0ST	1021 Cardiff	New South Wales Ry Transport Museum Thirlemere, Aus.
1915	1921	0-6-0ST	14 Charwelton	Kent & East Sussex Ry
2009	1921	0-6-0ST	41 Rhyl	Cholsey & Wallingford Railway
2010	1921	0-6-0ST	42 Rhonda	Caister Castle Museum
2015	1921	0-6-0ST	Abernant	Cholsey & Wallingford Railway
2018	1922	0-6-0ST	5 Littleton	Avon Valley Railway
2025	1923	0-6-0ST	Winston Churchill	Pensnett Trading Estate Shut End, West Midlands
2047	1926	0-6-0ST	Warwickshire	Severn Valley Railway

BIBLIOGRAPHY

References to Manning Wardle locomotives

Abbott, R.A.S. 1973 Crane Locomotives, A Survey of British Practice. 80pp
    Goose & Son, Publishing Ltd.

Ahrons, E.L. 1927 The British Steam Locomotive, 1825-1925, 391pp
    Locomotive Publishing Company, London.

Allan, I 1994 Industrial Steam. 80pp
    Ian Allan, London.

Allen, P.C. 1928 The Railways of the Isle of Wight, 84pp
    Locomotive Publishing Company, London.

Allen, P. & Wheeler, R. 1960 Steam on the Sierra.
    Cleaver-Hume Press Ltd, London

Atkins, P. 1996 Britain's most obscure locomotive, Blackpool
    Back Track, Jan., 1996. 40-41.

Armstrong, S 1996 The North Sunderland Railway
    Railway Bylines, Aug-Sept 1996, 2pp

Awdry, C. 1990 Encyclopaedia of British railway companies
    Patrick Stephens Ltd, Wellingborough.

Bagshawe, P.F. 1978 Some Industrial Locomotives of the K.D.L. in Zaire
    Industrial Railway Record No. 80, 7, 348-353.

Balfour, G. 1981. The Armoured Train.   B.T.Batsford Ltd, London

Bathurst, D. 1992 The Selsey Tram. 134 pp
    Phillimore, Chichester, Sussex.

Bennett, A.R. 1927 The Chronicles of Boulton's Siding, 272pp
    Locomotive Publishing Company, London.

Binns, D. 1995 The Anglo-Chilean Nitrate & Railway Company. 77pp
    Trackside Publications, Skipton, England

Boyd, J.I.C. 1949 Narrow gauge rails to Portmadoc. 158pp
    The Oakwood Press, Surrey.

Bradley, D.L. 1976 London & South Western Railway Album
    Ian Allan, London.

Brown, G.A., Prideaux, J.D.C.A., Radcliffe, H.G. 1971 (2nd ed.)
    The Lynton & Barnstaple Railway. 135 pp
    David & Charles, Newton Abbott
Buckle, K & Love, D 1994 British locomotives builder's plates. 80pp
    Midland Publishing Co., Leicester.
Butcher, A.C. 1995 Railways restored, 1995, a family guide
    Ian Allan, London.
Casserley, H.C. 1971 London & South Western Locomotives
    Ian Allan, London.
Chester, K. 1999 New Russia Co Ltd.
    Industrial Railway Record, No. 157, 146-154.
Clark, E.Kitson 1938   Kitsons of Leeds. 185pp
    Locomotive Publishing Company, London.
Coleford, I.C. 1996 Primus to Septimus - Furzebrook Clay Narrow
    Gauge. Railway Bylines, 12 pp, 23 illustrations.
Croxton, A.H. 1982 Railways of Zimbabwe
    David & Charles, Newton Abbott
Davies, W,J,K. 1981 The Ravenglass & Eskdale Railway
    David & Charles, Newton Abbot.
de Pater, A.D. & Page, F.M. 1987 Russian Locomotives. Vols 1 and 2
    Retrieval Press, Sutton Coldfield, England.
Emblin, R. 1993 Sir Berkeley & Friends, an impression of Manning Wardle's
    six-wheeled saddle tank engines. 19pp
    Vintage Carriage Trust, Keighley, N.Yorkshire.
Fisher, C. 1993 Industrial Locomotives of East Anglia
    Industrial Railway Society, London.
Gadsden, E.J.S. 1962 Duke of Buckingham's Railway
    Bledlow Press.
Gale, W.K.V. 1975 A History of the Pensnett Railway
    Goose and Son, Cambridge
Gammell, C.J. 1985 Relics of the Raj. 96pp
    G.R.Q. Publications, London
Garrett, C   1982   Preserved steam locomotives of Britain
    Blandford Press, Poole, Dorset.
Gradon, W.M. 1997 "Ratty", a history of the Ravenglass & Eskdake Railway
    Plateway Press, Norfolk.

Griffith, E. 1948 The West Sussex Railway. 42pp
    E.W.Langham, Farnham.
Hamilton Ellis, C. 1956 The South Western Railway. 256 pp
    George Allen & Unwin Ltd, London.
Hardy, C. 1982 E.B.Wilson & Co. 94pp
    Thomas Aleksandr, Birmingham.
Harris, M 1980 The British Narrow Gauge. 128pp
    Ian Allan, London.
Higgins, S.H.P. 1958 The Wantage Tramway
    The Abbey Press, Abingdon.
Hughes, H   1990 Indian Locomotives Part 1 Broad Gauge 1851-1940
            1992 Part 2 Metre Gauge 1872-1940
            1994 Part 3 Narrow Gauge 1863-1940
            1995 Part 4 1941-1990
    The Continental Railway Circle, Harrow, England
Jenkinson, D. & Lane, B.C. 1996 British Rail Cars. 81pp
    Atlantic Transport Publishers, Penrhyn, Cornwall.
Klapper, C. 1961 The Golden Age of Tramways. 327 pp
    Routledge & Kegan Paul, London.
Laursen, O. W. 1973. Bygone Light Railways of Europe. 154 pp
    The Oakwood Press,
Lewis, M.J.T. 1960 The Pentewan Railway, 1829-1919. 57pp
    D.B.Barton, Truro.
Lowe, J.W. 1975 British Steam Locomotive Builders. 704 pp
    Goose & Son, Cambridge.
Mabbott, F.W. 1981 Manning Wardle & Co. Ltd, locomotive works list
    288pp. Thomas Aleksandr, Birmingham.
Millichip, M. 1997 Samuel Williams & Sons, Dagenham Dock & Railways
    Railway Bylines, 2, 242-253. Irwell Press.
Nock, O.S. 1955 The Railway Engineers. 256pp
    Batsford, London.
Ottley, G. 1983 A Bibliography of British Railway History. 683pp
    Her Majesty's Stationery Office, London.
O'Connor, M.J. 1976 The Westland Works Railway, Yeovil.
    Industrial Railway Records, No.66, 232-236.

Palmer, A.N. & Stewart, W.W. Cavalcade of New Zealand Locomotives. 174pp
      Angus & Robertson, London.
Peters, I . 1976 The Narrow Gauge Charms of Yesterday
      Oxford Publishing Co.
Prideaux, J.D.C.A. 1978 The English Narrow Gauge Railway
      (A pictorial history) David & Charles, Newton Abbott.
Redman, R.N. 1972 The Railway Foundry, Leeds, 1839-1969
      Norwich.
Rolt, L.T.C. 1964 A Hunslet Hundred. 177pp
      David & Charles, Dawlish, Devon.
Russell, P. 1972 Steam in Camera (Photos of K.A.C.R.Nunn). 128pp
      Ian Allan, London.
Scott-Morgan, J. 1978 The Colonel Stephens Railways, 96pp
      Davis & Charles, Newton Abbott.
Simpson, B 1985   The Brill Tramway. 128pp
      Oxford Publishing Co.
Sawford, E. 1992 British Railways STEAM in the 1950s. 160pp
      Alan Sutton Publishing, Stroud, Glos.
Sawford, E. 1995 The last days of Industrial Steam. 156pp
      Alan Sutton Publishing, Stroud, Glos.
Smithers, M. 1992 Manning Wardle of Leeds. (11 illustrations)
      Backtrack 6, No.3 May-June 1992, 130-135.
Taylor, A.R, & Tonks, E.S. 1979 The Southwold Railway. 64pp
      Ian Allan, London.
Tilling, W.G. 1929 The Locomotives of the Southern Railway
      (Eastern Region). W.G.Tilling, London.
Tonks, E.S.   1948 The Edge Hill Light Railway
      E.S.Tonks, Birmngham.
Trevor Lowe, D. 1995 Narrow Guage Railways of Spain
          Vol. 1. Catalunga to the Sierra Nevade 96 pp
          Vol. 2. Castile to the Biscay Coast. 96 pp.
      Plateway Press, Brighton.
Usui, S. The Roots of Steam, steam locomotives in Japan, 1872-1972
      (in Japanese)
Wade, E.A. 1986 The Patent Narrow Gauge Railways of John Barraclough Fell
      Narrow Gauge Railway Society, 113, 1-36.

Warren, J.G.H. 1923 A Century of Locomotive Building by Robert Stephenson
    & Co 1823-1923. Andrew Reid & Co, Newcastle on Tyne.

Wells, J. 1993 Pig & Whistle Railway. (Knott End Ry)
    Back Track, Sept/Oct 1993, 257-265.

Whitcombe, H.A. 1954 History of a Steam Railway
    The Oakwood Press.

Whitehead, R.A. & Simpson, F.D. 1951 The Story of the Colne Valley
    Francis Ridgeway Ltd, Brentwood, Essex.

Whitehouse, P.B & Snell, J.B. 1984 Narrow Gauge Railways of the British Isles
    164pp. David & Charles, Newton Abbott.

Willingham, E.P. 1989 From Construction to Destruction (Colne Valley &
    Halsteam Ry). Halstead & District Historical Society, Halstead, Essex.

Woodcock, G. 1970 Minor Railways of England and their locomotives. 192pp
    Goose & Sons, Publishers, Norwich.

Wright, W.R. 1974 British owned railways in Argentina
    Austin.